Robert McLean AM is a Director Emeritus of McKinsey & Company. Having chaired The Nature Conservancy Australia for 20 years, he now serves as Vice Co-Chairman of TNC Asia Pacific. He is a former Dean of the Australian Graduate School of Management (UNSW), a founding trustee of McLean Foundation, a founding chair of Social Ventures Australia and a former director of Paul Ramsay Foundation. Robert became a member of the Order of Australia in 2011, and was awarded Philanthropy Australia's Life Time Achievement Award in 2021 and an Honorary Doctorate in Business from The University of New South Wales Business School in 2024.

Also by Robert McLean,
co-authored with Charles Conn

Bulletproof Problem Solving
The Imperfectionists

The Town Like No Other

A Story of Broken Hill

Robert McLean

First published in Australia in 2026 by Bakers Lane Books
www.bakerslane.com.au

Bakers Lane Books acknowledges the Traditional Owners of the Country on which we live and work. Our office is located on the lands of the Gadigal people of the Eora Nation. We pay our respects to all Aboriginal and Torres Strait Islander Elders, past and present.

A catalogue record for this book is available from the National Library of Australia

ISBN 978-1-7641321-2-1

Cover design by David Grant
Cover artwork: *Broken Hill Nocturne*, by Florence May Harding, Broken Hill City Art Gallery, © Estate of Florence May Harding, used with permission
Author photograph by Fancy Boy Photography
Map of Broken Hill and Surrounds by David Grant
Typeset by Midland Typesetters, Australia
Distributed by NewSouth Books
Printed and bound in Australia by Pegasus Media & Logistics

The paper in this book is FSC® certified. FSC® promotes environmentally responsible, socially beneficial and economically viable management of the world's forests.

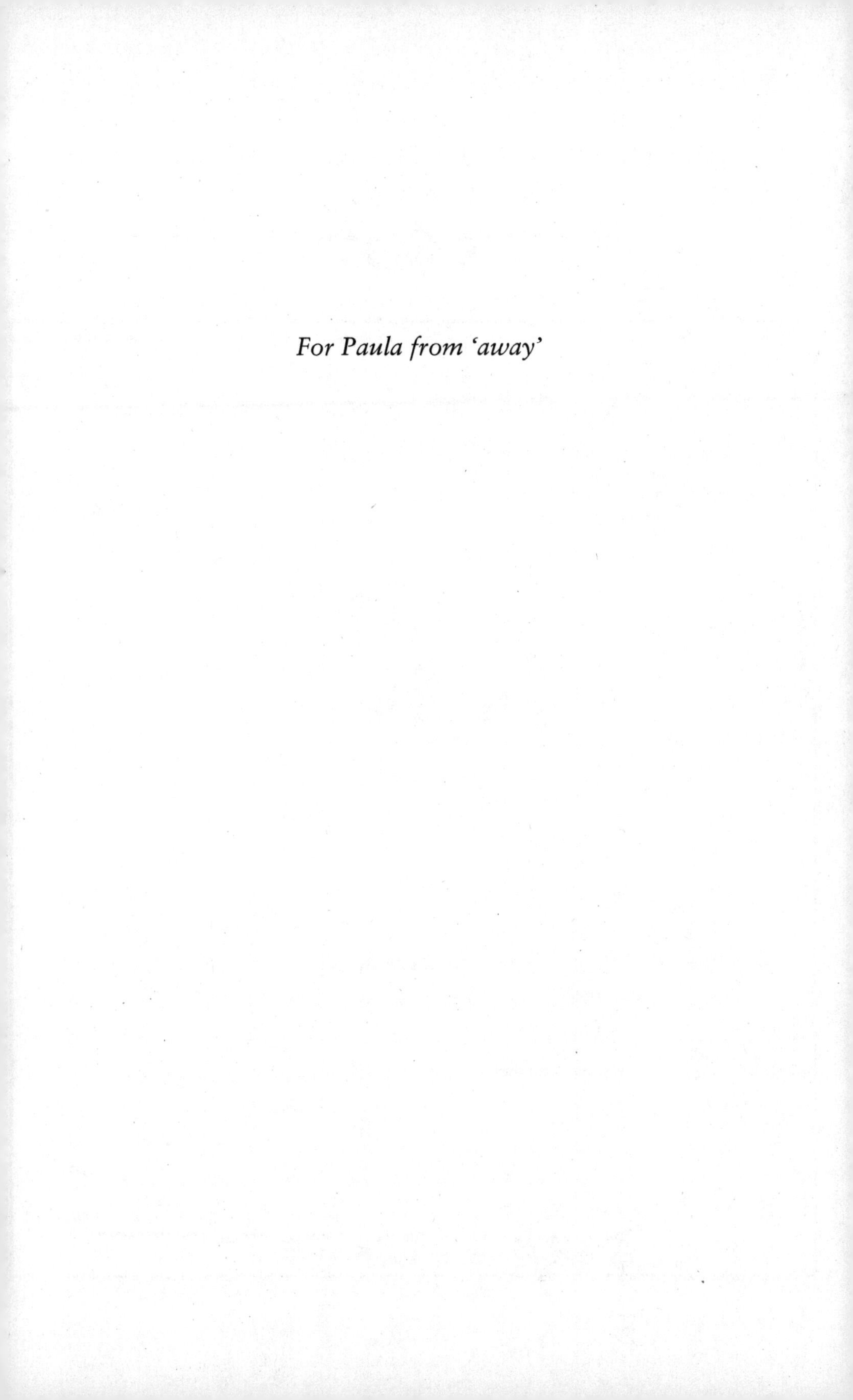

For Paula from 'away'

Map of Broken Hill and Surrounds

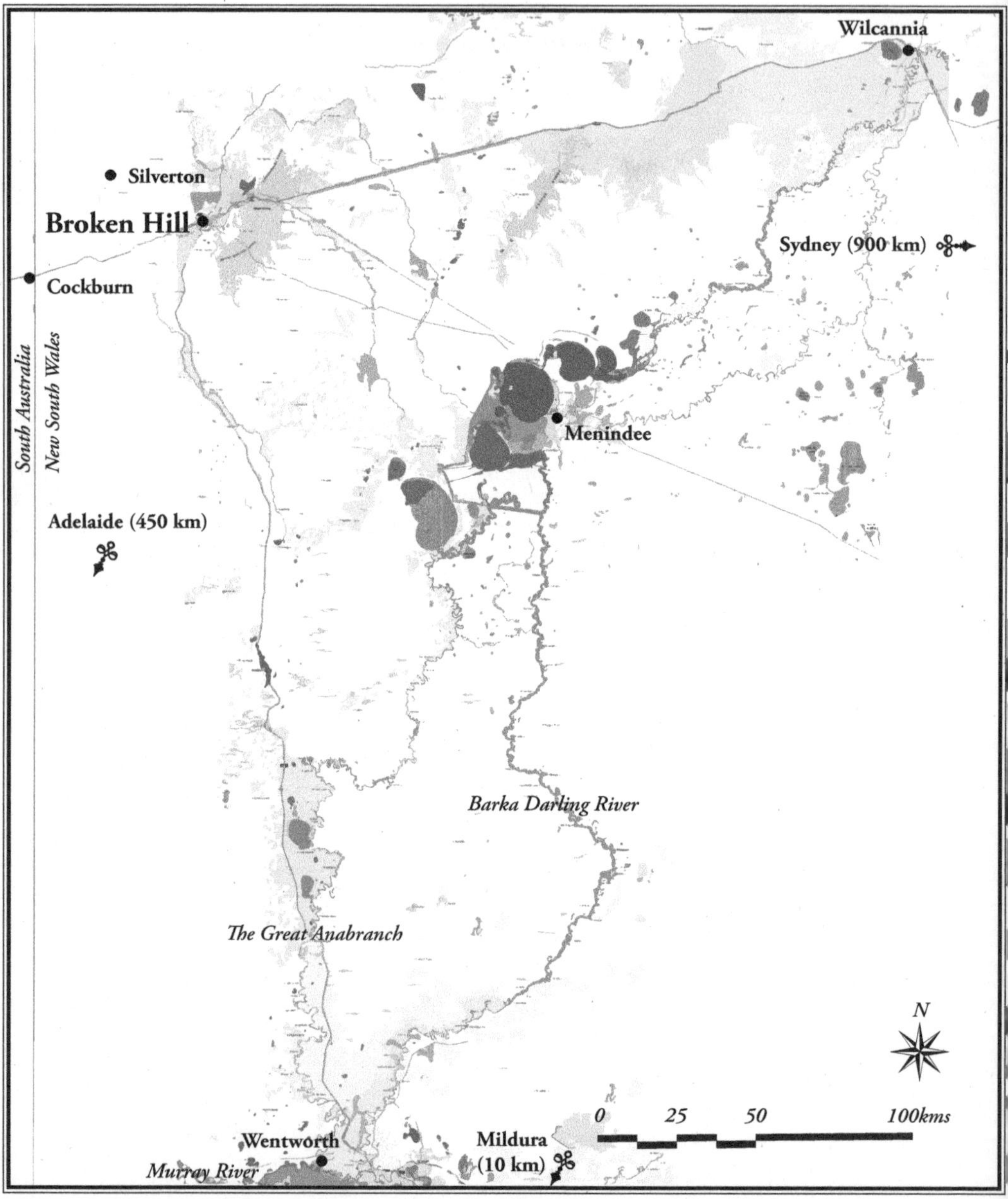

Wilcannia
Silverton
Broken Hill
Sydney (900 km)
Cockburn
South Australia
New South Wales
Menindee
Adelaide (450 km)
Barka Darling River
The Great Anabranch
N
0 25 50 100kms
Wentworth
Mildura (10 km)
Murray River

Contents

Prologue

The painting on the cover of this book, *Broken Hill Nocturne*, depicts a mountain of silver, zinc and lead tailings from decades of mining, what is called the line of lode. It looms over the outback town nestled below. It is the image every visitor to Broken Hill sees from its main streets, and it's the image the town's residents wake up to each day and carry with them throughout their lives.

May Harding painted *Broken Hill Nocturne* in 1967 and it is now in the Broken Hill City Art Gallery's permanent collection. I am indebted to May Harding's family who generously granted me permission to use the image.

It is the period between 1950 and 1970 that is the focus of the stories I tell in *The Town Like No Other* – the period when

I grew up in the town, where I received a first-class education at Broken Hill High School, and where I returned to after university to work at the Zinc Corporation, one of the town's mining companies. Much has been written of the town, with superb books like Geoffrey Blainey's *The Rise of Broken Hill.* However, not a great deal has been written of the time when the town was reaching its zenith.

I have come across many misconceptions of life in Broken Hill. Not surprisingly, these views were formed by people who did not live in the town, but who lived in our capital cities. Many of these misconceptions remain to this day. Depictions of industrial strife and long strikes, aloof mine managers concerned only with dividends to shareholders, insular outback residents living in insufferable heat and dust and working in unsafe conditions on the line of lode, are common. When asked where I went to school and I proudly say Broken Hill High School, I may as well have said, 'I went to an outback reform school.' Yet I was taught by highly trained teachers and large numbers of my graduating class went on to university. We were a long way away from the seats of government and this gave rise to Broken Hill finding local solutions and taking initiatives to solve problems.

This negative picture of Broken Hill butted up against my lived experience, and my pride. I saw mine managers and the unions locked in *mutual dependence*, where agreements were reached and each side could declare victory. They avoided strikes and both *won* financially. I enjoyed the benefits of corporate social responsibility by the mining companies, the likes of which

Australia hadn't seen before or since. I saw the outcome of mine managers and conservationists working together to reduce sand drifts and dust storms, establishing a protective regeneration area around the town. This was not common in other mining communities in Australia. I saw art become a way to foster an appreciation of an arid environment and become a building block that positioned Broken Hill as a tourist destination.

I found it hard to keep track of the number of community organisations the town had for its size. In my eyes we had rich social capital and a strong community. There was great civic pride in showing our town to visitors including Queen Elizabeth II on her brief visit in 1954. We were equally proud of local people who became successful in music, mining and sport, and who left Broken Hill to go on to bigger stages. We enjoyed being seen to punch above our weight.

Broken Hill was unusual in having the most Methodists and the most pubs of any city in Australia. It had numerous migrant groups making valued contributions. It was multicultural before we knew the word existed. It was a town of volunteers and joiners of civic organisations, with a budding artist community. It seemed like we had talent to burn in the 'Hill', and that talent was nurtured.

It was of course viewed as a *man's town*, renowned for drinking and gambling, and for its union control. But most townspeople at this time accepted this state of affairs, saying the unions had the best interests of the town at heart.

This 20-year timeframe is the heyday period of Broken Hill mining, when vast wealth was created, when miners were some of the best paid workers in Australia, when the population of the town swelled to 32,000. It was a period of industrial calm, record mine production and rapid productivity growth. It was also a period of record wool prices. Markets for minerals and wool peaked in the early 1950s, along with jobs, incomes and population growth. Arrangements hard fought for by unions in earlier decades, like collective bargaining and the lead bonus, were key to this prosperity.

However, it was also a time of a controversial 'social engineering' experiment by the Barrier Industrial Council (BIC) in effectively *running the town*. This finally came to an end in 1969 when the BIC decided to restrict their activities to industrial matters.

Within this magic-years history – my growing-up years – all was not idyllic of course. There was sadness and sorrow, in the landscape and in the hearts of people. Men died underground, women were deprived of opportunity, the land and rivers showed stress, and the mines began to run out.

I don't remember people talking about the treatment of Indigenous people when I was growing up. Indigenous people lived on the fringes, in the shadows of town life. This was a time when Indigenous children were still being removed from their families by the dreaded 'Protector'. In 1969 an Act of Parliament abolished the practice of child removal. And it wasn't until the late 1960s that mines started to offer jobs to Indigenous men and that schools began teaching Indigenous culture.

Prologue

To the question I've been asked thousands of times, 'What was it like to grow up in Broken Hill?' I now say, 'For me, my family and our friends, it was an inspirational and nurturing community. It fostered independence and allowed us to dream. It taught us to see the beauty of arid landscapes, and to understand both the fragility and the resilience of the land. It was the town like no other.'

Chapter 1

A Beautiful History

Robyn Ravlich, a highly awarded ABC radio broadcaster who grew up in Broken Hill much the same time as me, the 1950s and 1960s, describes her home town as having a 'beautiful history'. I was very taken with Robyn's marrying of *beautiful* and *history*, which she used when she signed my copy of her memoir, *Skywriting*, at her book launch in 2019. Robyn is of Croatian Australian parentage and the beautiful history she was referring to includes stories of multiculturalism, community engagement, social capital and educational opportunity. These aspects of growing up in this semi-arid remote mining town have been given scant attention by writers of the town's history – yet it is these very aspects of a town's health and cohesion that contribute to positive outcomes for its citizens and their children.

I was curious about this term, a beautiful history, and turned to Perplexity and Google. I discovered that sociologists use it to refer to the lived experiences of people in the past, in particular those of ordinary people, looking at their culture, how they socialise in their community, and what is uplifting and inspiring about their experiences.

I share Robyn's fondness for growing up in Broken Hill and believe this was also the case for the majority of the 30,000 residents for the two decades from 1950. This shared history is one of many stories that contribute to my naming this book *The Town Like No Other*.

WHAT MAKES FOR A BEAUTIFUL HISTORY?

Broken Hill's heyday period, the fifties and sixties, I believe, began with a dilemma and how that dilemma was resolved in the community. Actors great and small played a critical role in creating this heyday period of history, and without the foresight and determination of the key players, the town's history would have been very different.

In Broken Hill's case, the dilemma was how the mines could share the wealth from a world-class orebody, a dilemma resolved by growing the economic pie and providing much larger slices to all in a way not seen before. A key decision was to avoid the historical trend of frequent strikes in previous periods, even though there was a continuous to-and-fro between the unions and the mine managers for authority. By working together, avoiding strikes, they found a way. The positive outcomes were well-paid jobs, wealth shared equitably among stakeholders and excellent educational opportunities. The actors great and small include the Barrier Industrial Council (BIC) chief Shorty O'Neil and mine managers like Maurie Mawby, Robert Pitman Hooper and Jack Liebelt, all from Zinc Corporation, as well as what philosopher Edmund Burke called the all-important 'little platoons'. Families, churches and community organisations were among the little platoons.

I'm struck by how many people who grew up in Broken Hill in this period describe feeling a great sense of freedom – even though this sense of freedom was tempered by living within the 'walled city' rules of the BIC regarding prices and employment. This sense of personal freedom that we felt came in part from the town's isolation, some 1150 kilometres from the State's capital, Sydney. Government in all forms and bureaucracy played a very small role in our lives. The town just got on with it, identifying what was important and needed for their community.

An important measure of a person's potential comes from having a job with adequate income. Broken Hill had essentially full employment from 1950–70. Miners' incomes were high relative to those of professionals in capital cities. One wage from a miner working a 35-hour week was adequate to support a family, although married women were denied this opportunity under BIC rules, in the interest of keeping unmarried young women in Broken Hill.

Along with a secure job and a good income to mine employees went a slew of community investments by the mines in ovals, parks, clubs, and hospital and dental care. It was a level of investment that was unprecedented in Australia. It was a prime example of corporate social responsibility made by the directors of the four mining companies. They had a keen eye on their role to advance shareholders' interests. The result was that the companies and the community prospered in this period. Later, as a mine's life and profitability came under pressure, the mine managers sought to wind back payments to the City Council and the generous lead bonus payments to mine employees, a form of profit sharing based on the price of lead.

The mines were becoming safer in the 1950s and 1960s. Mine managers elevated the importance of safe work practices and working in safe conditions. They were able to demonstrate that increased production didn't need to come at the expense of safety. In 1952 there were no fatalities recorded on the line of lode, the first year in its history. The next year without a fatality wasn't until 1981. When a siren alerted us to a fatality, silence followed as men took a day off under union rules. I call it the sounds of silence.

Faith and fraternity were strong in Broken Hill. Ironically, they came in the form of polar opposites: church attendance and pub going. Broken Hill was principally a town of Methodists and Roman Catholics who made up over 60 per cent of the population in 1954. Methodists were better known for joyful hymns than promoting temperance, but pubs flourished as miners had good pay and short working hours. Although the twin elements of faith and fraternity contributed to a strong sense of belonging for men, this wasn't especially shared by women. I can't ever recall my mother, a Methodist, going to the Ladies Lounge of a pub.

The wide range of community organisations in Broken Hill also contributed to a sense of belonging. I describe the town as being so rich in social capital that it compared favourably with any other similar town in Australia and the United States. The community organisations supported everything from education and sporting interests, to helping those in need. It was a town of volunteer joiners, the likes of which we hadn't seen before, enabled by the short working week and high incomes. It continued a tradition of self-reliance that went back 50 years when the people of Broken Hill realised that relying on the New South Wales Government to solve local problems meant you'd be waiting a long time. My parents were typical of Broken Hill adults participating in the community, my mother with Red Cross and Meals on Wheels, my father with the P&C, the annual flower show at the Zinc Lakes and the Masonic Club.

Although small in numbers, migrant communities made important contributions to town life and many migrants emerged as civic leaders. English language classes held at the high school and the Pig and Whistle pub helped. Sporting leaders also emerged from migrant families.

Most people would have a picture of miners and conservationists having opposing interests. However, the success of the revegetation of the area around Broken Hill showed that there were common interests between miners and conservationists. The natural environment of Broken Hill suffered greatly from mining and grazing. Photos of the woodfired smelters belching smoke tell a story, as do those of hundreds of rabbits surrounding a waterhole. The loss of native vegetation led to frequent sand drifts and dust storms. Miners and conservationists, led by Albert Morris of the Barrier Field Naturalists Club, collaborated to address the issue. They planted a green belt of native plants and trees around the perimeter of the city. The green belt was fenced to keep out rabbits, sheep and goats, and came to be known as the Regeneration Area. It was a resounding success in stopping sand drifts encroaching on houses and the mine structures.

The Menindee Pipeline in 1952 and the Lakes Scheme in 1960 solved Broken Hill's need for a reliable water supply. An unfortunate side effect was that it reduced flows to the Anabranch, the ancient river, where we had once been able to catch Murray Cod and yabbies. Only at the end of the 1960s did we come to appreciate the significance of the Barka, the Barkindji name for the Darling River. At the same time, the Indigenous history of the region started to be told and efforts were made to protect rock art and sacred sites of the people of Mutawintji.

Finally, in the late sixties, Aboriginal men were offered jobs as miners. The Indigenous people of the West Darling lived on the margins of Broken Hill, at Silverton, Menindee and Wilcannia. They lived lives in parallel to mine, some still escaping the Protector until 1969 when the controversial Act was repealed.

A love of the arid landscape was being expressed by a growing number of artists who formed the Willyama Art Society in 1962. We came to see beauty in the paintings of native plants and flowers, twisted mulga trees and the dry creek beds surrounding the town. An art teacher, Florence May Harding – whose painting *Broken Hill Nocturne* is on the cover of this book – played a key role in teaching many of the town's artists. In time Broken Hill came to be called the art capital of the outback.

The excellent education system at Broken Hill High School played a crucial role in developing the potential of its students at this time. In 1963, 50 per cent of its students went on to tertiary education, a level made possible by expanding scholarships and teaching opportunities. Many of my classmates earned university degrees in science and mining, combining work with study.

Broken Hill continued to punch above its weight in exporting talent, and not just in producing many mining engineers. There was a substantial talent pool in the arts, science and sport. We felt we could compete with the best in Australia. Although in sport, we sometimes got a reality check when competing with the best, like our loss to the Melbourne Demons in 1968 on the Jubilee Oval in North Broken Hill!

A beautiful history is not without 'flaws in the glass'. Not everyone would describe their growing-up years as a beautiful history, in particular the Indigenous people of Broken Hill and surrounding towns. Nor would the families who lost husbands or sons on the line of lode, or young married women who were denied the opportunity to work for half a century. Or the isolated mothers desperately reaching out to Lifeline.

LENSES FOR LOOKING AT THE PAST

I have come to see history through several lenses. The first lens is that of 'history as wonder', the idea of feeling curious and having a desire to know something about a time and place that is somewhat unlike popularly held beliefs.[1] The lens leads me to a different set of perspectives than that of friends and acquaintances who questioned me about life in Broken Hill. I think it's important to set the record straight, to balance the ledger and argue the case for a storyline based on the reality so many experienced at this time.

Another lens is rational inquiry, which comes from analysing data. This lens is one I'm always eager to use with my training in economics and statistics and a lifetime of problem-solving in business and community. I have used questions and hypotheses to test against the evidence. In many cases I have been surprised by what I've found. An example is the popular belief that unions got the better of management.

There are many books and documents I've had the privilege to draw on.[2] I am indebted to many chroniclers of Broken Hill's past, particularly historians Geoffrey Blainey, Robert Solomon and Ross Kearns. Jenny Camilleri has cast a light on the contributions of women while Bobbie Hardy is the only writer to focus on Indigenous people around Broken

Hill. Newer sources such as the *Australian Women's Register* and the online profiles of *Heroes, Larrikins and Visionaries* of Broken Hill have been especially useful.

The final lens I use is that of storytelling, providing a narrative from personal observation and conversations with many people. I have personal memories of South's footy club being a paragon of multiculturalism. As a young man I would see my dad and uncle Alister dressed formally on a weeknight, heading off to the Masonic Temple, one of the many organisations that made up civil society in Broken Hill. I also recall my mother going to Meals on Wheels to provide lunch for those in need. They were part of the rich social capital built in the town. I have been able to draw on recollections of many friends and classmates who also lived in Broken Hill. School magazines, football team photos and personal experiences of classmates have been an invaluable resource. My father's memoirs and essays left to our family are sources I return to time and again for his historical view and perspective.

A Century of Our Family in the Hill

Our family have an unbroken 125-year tie to Broken Hill. My grandfathers, Kenneth McLean and Alexander Alan Aldrich, arrived in Broken Hill around 1900. Grandfather McLean came from Scotland via Adelaide. Grandfather Aldrich came from Cunnamulla via Mount Browne. Grandpa McLean was a pipefitter and security officer who worked for almost 50 years with BHP in Broken Hill and

Whyalla. He was rewarded for heroism in his efforts to find four men who died underground. Grandpa Aldrich had his own butcher shop in Blende Street, across the road from his home. Both men met their wives in Broken Hill. My mother, Audrey Aldrich, and my father, Frank McLean MM, were both born in Broken Hill. I grew up there with my brother Ian and sister Judith.

At one point in the 1950s we had an extended family of 25 living in the town. We celebrated birthdays and holidays with family picnics at places like The Gorge. My dad was close to his brother Alister, a shift boss and safety training officer at Zinc Corporation. Dad's sister was Nellie Williams. Her son Jim was the first person in our family to go to university in about 1958. My mother Audrey was close to her three sisters Rita, Mary and Una. Mary's daughter Helen Giblett is the only family member who continues to live in Broken Hill.

My father was fond of saying, 'You have to live in the Hill, be a part of it to really understand it. Once you leave the Hill you become an "away" person to those who remain.' Strictly speaking, I'm an 'away' person to today's residents of Broken Hill. But I still identify as a boy who grew up in the Hill. I return as often as I can for school reunions and holidays with my wife Paula. We always visit the Broken Hill City Art Gallery, the Miners Memorial on the line of lode, and my cousin Helen and friend Vic Seekamp at Woolcunda Station near the Great Anabranch of the Barka Darling River.

MYTHS AND REALITY

Growing up in Broken Hill we understood how the town worked. Outsiders had contrary views, like Donald Horne with his scathing criticisms of how life was controlled in Broken Hill by the BIC. As I've researched how the town was viewed, by insiders and outsiders, I've come across many myths that stand in contrast to reality.

Outsiders would often say to me, 'Broken Hill has lots of strikes.' That was true in 1919 and 1920 but in the two decades from 1950–69, the mining companies lost only 10 days to strikes out of 4800 working days (excluding the 50 or so days lost after a mine fatality). There was also the view that the BIC got what they wanted in negotiations with the Mine Managers Association. The facts are that miners received exceptional pay and conditions in the 1950s and 1960s. At the same time the mining companies reached production targets, earned reasonable returns on capital, generated cash flow to open new mines and achieved a productivity growth rate twice as high as the rest of Australia.

In the social domain the town's reputation for having pubs open at all hours, as well as two-up games and pokies, led visitors to frown on the people of Broken Hill. Many didn't visit long enough to appreciate that this unique community was what today we would call 'rich in social capital', a town of volunteers and joiners, from active Parents and Citizens Associations to repertory, field naturalists and pipe bands. This was an era in which miners worked a 35-hour week, the highest percentage of car ownership in Australia made travel to an evening function easy, and television was still 16 years away.

Negotiations between the Mine Managers Association and the BIC is now more easily explained by negotiation theory – 'that each depended on the other'. The theory wasn't developed until 1960, then primarily in relation to nuclear warfare with the notion of *mutual dependence*.[3] This came about from feelings of mutual respect, together with a collective bargaining framework that was already running smoothly by 1950.

The incredible community investment in social and sporting facilities experienced in Broken Hill during this period has come to be called 'corporate social responsibility' or CSR. At the time it was unparalleled in Australia.

A-, B- AND C-GROUPERS

Are you an A-grouper? This was the defining question for the men of Broken Hill. A man who was either born or educated in Broken Hill, or had lived there for eight years, was an A-grouper. The concept of B-groupers was proposed by the mining companies in order to expand the labour pool. B-groupers were men who were born within 482 kilometres (300 miles) of the town. The inclusion of B-groupers in the workforce resulted in a six-day strike in 1950, but the exclusive domain of mine work for A-groupers ended. C-groupers were people 'from away', outside the town and beyond the B-grouper catchment area.

I am an A-grouper, as were my father and my grandfathers. Because Dad was an A-grouper, he was supported by the BIC to be employed at Zinc Corporation when he returned to Broken Hill from Whyalla in 1950. Long after leaving the town, as a board member of Pacific Dunlop, I was introduced to a group of Melbourne businesspeople by John Ralph. John had been Chief Executive of Con Zinc Rio Tinto Australia. He simply said, 'Rob's an A-grouper.' I felt a great sense of belonging despite the exclusivity issue. Today an A-grouper proposal would immediately be challenged as a discriminatory practice in labour law.

Your identification as an A- or B-grouper was one of many fault lines in Broken Hill. You were either 'from the Hill' or 'from away'. You were most likely either Methodist or Roman Catholic. You worked in town or on the mines. You were either union or staff. You were an unmarried woman and could work, or a married woman who couldn't. You were from either 'the South', north Broken Hill, the central part of town, or you were a westie. This effectively defined which of the town's Australian Rules teams you supported. These seemingly cavernous divides disappeared when we had dealings with government or people 'from away'. Then we would close ranks and identify as coming from 'the Hill'.

There is an expression that history doesn't feel like history when you are going through it. That was the case for me as a boy and as a university graduate returning to work in Broken Hill in the late sixties. Our family and community were all important. We enjoyed simple pleasures. Most of all we grew up to see a world of opportunity through education, feeling supported in my case with a mines scholarship and confidence that I could hold my own anywhere.

When you look at Broken Hill through the lens of curiosity and the lofty lens of human development, you get to see something different and something quite special. During these years Broken Hill was the town like no other on so many dimensions – it was a moment in time, which has lasted in parts, but where the whole is unlikely to be seen again. To me it meets all the requirements to be called a beautiful history.

Chapter 2

The 'Broken Hill'

> Broken Hill in 1888 was new and raw and vital. High wages and higher hopes brought a riotous inrush ... the town's streets were thronged with share jobbers and confidence men, brawny miners and staid businessmen ... there were 26 hotels and rather fewer churches ... lead smelters turned night into day.[1]
>
> *Bobbie Hardy*

From its very entrepreneurial beginnings, Broken Hill became a world-class and a world-scale mining province, a major town in Australia, and a place where battles were fought between ideologies relating to labour and the shareholders' interest.

THE ORIGIN STORY: 1883–1905

The 'broken hill' was a feature in the landscape that attracted attention. The original name for the town of Broken Hill was Willyama, meaning a hill with a broken contour in the Wilyakali language of the Indigenous people. Mount Gipps sheep station nearby had a paddock called the 'broken hill' paddock. It was a boundary rider on Mount Gipps Station, Charles Rasp, who came across the unusual outcrop, believing it to be tin. Explorer Captain Charles Sturt was travelling through the Barrier Ranges in 1844 and made mention of the 'broken hill'.

Rasp pegged out a mining lease on the 'broken hill' with the mines surveyor at Silverton. He then decided to tell the Mount Gipps station manager and part-owner, George McCulloch, of his action. That evening they talked about Rasp's discovery and McCulloch proposed a syndicate of seven to take leases on the remaining six blocks. The syndicate of seven weren't your typical mining prospectors. They included a sheep overseer, a storekeeper, a station hand, and an owner of bullock teams as well as Charles Rasp and George McCulloch.[2] Each syndicate member contributed 70 pounds – equivalent to $15,000 today. With this money they were able to peg out more leases. In the historical accounts we hear nothing of the Wilyakali people's rights to the land. There was no native title, only mining law.

Capital was needed to develop the mineral prospects, so the syndicate took the decision to float a limited company.

The new company, the Broken Hill Proprietary Company Limited, was registered in Melbourne on 13 August 1885. Rasp and McCulloch retained their shareholdings and became wealthy men. McCulloch added to his shareholding in 1884 by buying a share from a station hand. In six months, the share was worth what would amount to over $250 million today.[3] Others joined in forming companies near the BHP leases. Some of the mining companies had unimaginative names like Block 10. But there were colourful mine names like Gipsy Girl, Lady Brassey and Cosgrove's Dream. It was a time of extraordinary fortune and speculation, and the birth of BHP, one of the world's great resource companies.

In 1889 the population of Broken Hill was 10,000, and two years later it had doubled to nearly 20,000. This made it the second largest population centre in New South Wales.

THE LINE OF LODE

The resource was a massive silver, lead and zinc orebody, estimated at between 200 and 250 million tonnes of ore before mining, with lead and zinc grades of 15 to 25 per cent.[4] In the first few years of operation, the Broken Hill mines provided one third of the annual silver produced worldwide. By the outbreak of World War I, Broken Hill was the world's largest exporter of lead, and supplied 6 per cent of the world's silver and about 20 per cent of the world's annual zinc production.[5]

The line of lode refers to the shape of the Broken Hill orebody. It looks like a coat hanger, a saddle or even a boomerang – a 'coat hanger' that is 7.5 kilometres across and reaches down to 1.6 kilometres in depth. The BHP leases were in the middle of the line of lode closest to the surface. They were the first to be worked and among the first to be worked out. At either extremity of the line of lode were the deep mines of North Broken Hill and Zinc Corporation and New Broken Hill Consolidated. Geology was destiny for leaseholders on the line of lode.

BHP was well positioned in the early days of mining the line of lode. However, their future was limited as the ore ran out at 500 metres. Besides BHP there was the Central mine of Sulphide Corporation, then Broken Hill South. Later Zinc Corporation was to take up the leases to process tailings in 1905, followed by New Broken Hill Consolidated taking up the southernmost leases. On the northern side of BHP was its Block 14, a separately floated company, then the British and Junction mines, the Junction North and finally North Broken Hill. The latter mine, like Zinc Corporation/New Broken Hill Consolidated, at the other end of the line of lode, had decades of reserves after BHP finished mining in 1939.

But after the first decade of mining a serious problem arose. The recovery processes were fine for silver and lead but left much of the zinc in the tailings. BHP hired a General Manager, G.D. Delprat, with a background in metallurgy and engineering. He experimented with a flotation process to recover zinc, which after litigation in 1902 became known as the Potter-Delprat process.

In 1904 the Mines Department estimated that there were 5.7 million tons of tailings containing zinc, and the tailings problem came to be seen as an opportunity, when the first sales of zinc concentrate were made. Herbert Hoover, later to become President of the United States, visited in 1905 as a mining entrepreneur together with Francis Govett, co-managing director of Zinc Corporation. Hoover acquired 400,000 tons of tailings and options on a further 3.5 million tons.[6] Hoover and his partners at Zinc Corporation had enough confidence about zinc recovery efforts to warrant the financial outlay. Their investment made Broken Hill an innovation centre in metallurgy for decades to come.

Growing up in Broken Hill we went on mine tours where we learned the history of zinc recovery by flotation. I didn't appreciate that early in the twentieth century a technology revolution of great significance was playing out in our home town. The contributors to the flotation innovation went beyond Delprat and Potter. They included men with very different perspectives on the problem, such as Auguste deBavay, a Melbourne brewer, F.J. Lyster who was trained as a carpenter, and Leslie Bradford who had diplomas in mining, metallurgy and chemistry. Numerous experiments were undertaken and results logged to see the effect on zinc recoveries. One experiment added eucalyptus, a well-known Australian 'cure all', producing 'sensational effects'.[7] The knowledge was shared with all the mining companies, making patents available to all mines.

From the beginning, BHP thought big about the world-class mineral province they had found. As the leading company in the field, they sought out the best mining talent in the world. W.H. Patton joined in September 1887. Patton was the former head of the famous Comstock silver lode in Nevada that had been discovered in 1859. He was the inventor of the square set timber stoping method. Square set stoping is a method of underground mining where the walls and back of the rockface are supported by interlocking framed timbers. The method was ideally suited for achieving high ore recovery in high grade underground mines like BHP, but one that required filling the spaces between the timber frames.[8]

Patton was followed by mine manager S.R. Wilson. He proposed the open cut method in 1891, the largest of its kind in the world. It was almost a mile long and 100 metres deep and produced 1.4 million tons of ore over 15 years.

I remember seeing the open cut as a boy and looking at it with wonder. The pungent smell of sulphur plumes from zinc sulphide burning in the open cut smelled like the rotten egg gas that we produced in the chemistry lab at high school.

Managing mines requires technical leadership and people leadership. Technical leadership was clearly evident in mining and metallurgy. But there was an equally demanding task of people leadership. By 1891 mine employment swelled to 5800 men. Miners had fears for their health with the exposure to lead and the inadequate safety conditions underground. Fatal accidents were a part of Broken Hill mining from the beginning. Between 1888 and 1899 there were 123 fatalities, roughly 10 deaths each year. The decade to 1909 was worse with 178 fatalities. The fatalities were attributed to unstable rock leading to rock falls, and a lack of safety consciousness and safe behaviour by miners.

In 1890 being a miner was not only a safety hazard but a health hazard. There were 98 cases of plumbism – lead poisoning – and 123 in the following year. In 1892 a Board of Inquiry was set up to investigate plumbism. The collection of statistics on the incidence of lead poisoning began in 1895 and three years later lead poisoning cases fell to two for every thousand men. The risks weren't confined to underground miners as 28 smelters were operating in 1892. The BHP smelter was closed in 1898 and other closures followed soon after. People leadership by the mine managers was being tested beyond ore production and concentrate.

LABOUR VERSUS CAPITAL: 1892–1920

Strikes were defining moments in the industrial history of Broken Hill. The 'great strike' in 1892 lasted 18 weeks, the strike in 1909 went for 20 weeks and the 'long strike' (sometimes called the 'big strike') in 1919–20 for 18 months.

The great strike was the name given to the first large strike on the Broken Hill mining field. In 1892 a recession followed metal price falls. Mine managers were looking to cut costs to remain profitable and pay dividends. They came up with the idea of contract mining – that is, paying miners in relation to ore tonnage. The union, the Amalgamated Miners Association, opposed 'stoping by contract' and sought to prohibit non-union labour and prevent 'free labour' from Melbourne arriving and taking jobs. BHP biographer Roy Bridges termed it a 'mine owner's victory' when the men returned to work.[9] The New South Wales Government arrested the strike leader Richard Sleath and six others. Six men were jailed for two months to two years. While BHP declared a productivity boost from contract stoping and the use of subcontractors on the open cut, historian Brian Kennedy concluded, '[I]f it did not create the deep divisions between the unions and companies it now rendered them a permanent feature of the town.'[10]

The lengthy 1892 strike led to hardship in the town. The Broken Hill Benevolent Society, the only recognised charitable organisation, operated out of the courthouse.[11] The society had a committee of 24, 12 men and 12 women, and a secretary. Broken Hill was divided into 12 districts. The society distributed over $120,000 in food, with all the work being done by volunteers. Social services were undeveloped in Australia in 1892, so it's not surprising that Broken Hill came forward with a community-based model.

The 1909 strike was also brought on by the fall in price of silver, lead and zinc. The mines were making little or no profit and proposed reverting to the wage levels of two years earlier. Justice Higgins, famous for introducing the basic wage concept in the Harvester agreement, ruled that BHP couldn't cut wages when workers' costs had increased with inflation. Tom Mann, a socialist who organised the London Dock Strike, arrived on the scene and opened negotiations with Delprat,

BHP's General Manager, seeking to avoid penalties for strike leaders and to have recognition of the union, the Amalgamated Miners' Association (AMA). The strike ended in May. Geoffrey Blainey concluded that '... to some historians unions had suffered total defeat at Broken Hill but in reality they had won'.[12] They had won because wage reductions by individual mines could no longer be proposed by mine management.

In Geoffrey Blainey's view the long strike of 1919–20 '... began with disputes that seemed trivial'.[13] There was a big divide in expectations, between what the unions wanted and what the mines needed to remain profitable. Compensation and lung disease were the trigger issues of the long strike.

The New South Wales Government responded to union concerns about lead poisoning and pneumoconiosis with the Chapman Commission, which provided its findings in July 1920. Once again, an arbiter was appointed. This time it was Justice Edmunds. His recommendations were to have profound effects for decades to come:

- Union membership as a requirement to work on the mines other than staff roles.
- A 35-hour week underground and no night shift.
- Testing of miners' lungs for TB and pneumoconiosis.
- One wage structure across the line of lode.
- Contract stoping of ore – opposed by unions but retained.

BHP's Long Goodbye

BHP had a long goodbye from Broken Hill, from the early days to the time it finally stopped operations in 1939. It went from being the 'big mine' in 1889 to one of several when it left. BHP's General Manager Guillaume Delprat didn't share the confidence of Zinc Corporation Director W.S. Robinson about Broken Hill's future. Robinson states that in 1907 Delprat advised against a new building for the Broken Hill Club as mine life would be finished in seven to 10 years.[14] BHP's focus had moved to building a steel industry by 1911.

BHP was an integral part of my family's life in Broken Hill. In 1950 my grandfather Ken McLean completed almost 50 years of service with BHP in Broken Hill and Whyalla. He was celebrated for heroism in a tragic mine gas incident in 1935. My father started work with BHP in 1934; a few years later he transferred to BHP's Whyalla shipyard before the outbreak of World War II. He made the point in his memoirs that BHP's leaving Broken Hill '... brought applause as they were *cordially hated* by the people of Broken Hill'.

COLLECTIVE BARGAINING AND MUTUAL DEPENDENCE: 1921–30

In 1920 Justice Edmunds recommended that a collective bargaining process between the mining companies and unions be put in place with an industrial agreement. It was out of this agreement that the lead bonus was introduced in 1925. It was to have a huge effect on miners' income levels in the 1950s.

Two men played a critical role in the aftermath of the long strike of 1919–20. One was union leader Paddy O'Neill who became the first head of the Barrier Industrial Council (BIC) when it was created as a peak body. O'Neill served as BIC President until his retirement in 1949. The other was Mine Managers' Association (MMA) President Andrew Fairweather. Labour historians Ellem and Shields credit the 1935 industrial agreement led by O'Neill and Fairweather for '... providing the foundations of long-term material prosperity for Broken Hill mine workers'.[15] In a tribute to Fairweather on his retirement the union newspaper, the *Barrier Daily Truth*, had this to say about O'Neill and Fairweather:

> Fairweather (MMA President) and (Paddy) O'Neill (BIC) each played an important part in the development of the line of lode and the development of happier industrial relations in this city, and it can be said that their efforts were mutually beneficial for both the workers and their companies, for each was shrewd enough to know *that the welfare of the one depended on the other*.[16]
> [emphasis added]

The unions were interested in pay and conditions for existing employees rather than maximising employment. The mine managers were seeking high levels of uninterrupted production. This provided an envelope of mutual interest. There were implications for how the mines were run. With the costs of employees largely fixed, other than for contract miners, the incentive is to produce as much ore as possible with the available workforce. Safety and miners' health were now an important part of mine management responsibility. Big reductions in the fatality rate were made from 1920 to 1949 as safety consciousness became a formal responsibility of mine management.

THE GREAT DEPRESSION: 1929–39

Broken Hill was hit hard by the Great Depression. Silver, lead and zinc prices did not return to 1929 levels until 1940 when World War II began. Employment levels on the mines fell 46 per cent between 1929 and 1931. They didn't return to the 1929 level until 1947, post-World War II. Wages were basically unchanged through the 1930s at roughly $250 per week (in today's dollars), only an 8 per cent increase in almost a decade. The community rallied with soup kitchens and relief for those in need.

Unemployment statistics aren't available for that time but they were likely to be similar to the rest of Australia, at over 20 per cent. In 1930, in response to shrinking job opportunities, the BIC introduced a policy to ban married women from working in jobs other than those specified like nursing and teaching. The policy was to last for the next 50 years.

Depression Era Memories

There are many colourful stories in my own family that describe life in Broken Hill during the Great Depression. My father left school at 14 to help provide for his family. He supplemented his income at BHP by working as an usher at the movie theatres on weekends. Dad told stories of catching rabbits and shooting galahs for food for the family. He especially enjoyed telling the story that they cooked the galah in hot stones and when it was ready you gnawed on the stone. As children our eyes would get very wide! Another of my father's budget specials was a pig's foot encased in gelatine, called a 'pig's trotter'.

When my father talked about how difficult the Great Depression was, he sometimes told us of the 'Chateau de tar drums' in West Broken Hill. Shanties were made from tar drums as shelter for unemployed men. While the 'Chateau' may have been the worst example of poverty, a considerable amount of the housing stock was substandard in Broken Hill.

NEW BEGINNINGS: 1936–49

A new beginning was marked in 1936 with the announcement to develop the NBHC mine at the southern end of the line of lode. W.S. Robinson, then Managing Director of Zinc Corporation, had this to say:

> When the world slowly lifted itself out of the depression and the prices of zinc and lead rose again, I decided it was time to explore vigorously the southern ground. For this purpose we floated a new company, known as New Broken Hill Consolidated Limited (NBHC), in London in 1936.[17]

WS, as Robinson was called, predicted that Broken Hill would be operating in 50 years' time.[18] Along with the new mine announcement went measures to address mining's impact on the environment and initiatives to build the community. The announcement was bold, innovative and unprecedented. W.S. Robinson goes on to criticise himself and his fellow directors for neglecting the living standards of people in the town.

The war years remained difficult for the mines with employment at around 3500 jobs. It was only in the period from 1945–49 that employment recovered strongly to 5861 jobs.

During this period the combination of a weak labour market and a collective bargaining regime meant that industrial action was subdued. Mine output and productivity were at the same level in 1949 as they had been in 1925. Collective bargaining may have built trust and avoided strikes but it hadn't translated into productivity gains, essential for long-term competitiveness. The benefits from changes in mining methods, mechanisation and the stabilisation of mined areas were all about to come to fruition in the next decade and provide a productivity lift.

In summing up the first half century of Broken Hill mining, historian Geoffrey Blainey says, 'The genius which the companies had displayed in solving their metallurgical and marketing problems was invisible when they faced labour problems.'[19]

It took another generation in the period from 1920–49 to demonstrate that mining, technology and labour could be managed to the highest order, with safety at the core of mining operations. After a collective bargaining approach was forced on the mine managers and the unions, it evolved into an extremely effective way to align their interests.

Chapter 3

The Magic Years

> The townspeople went through a magic period ... the late forties, fifties and sixties were wonderful years for the town.
>
> *Frank McLean, personal memoirs*

My father wrote these words when he was in his sixties. He was describing Broken Hill in its heyday, the time when he and my mother were raising three children. I haven't heard anyone else describe this period in Broken Hill's history in this way, and his use of the term *the magic period* spurred me on to write this book. I set out to gather facts and stories that would confirm my father's description – a description that mirrored Robyn Ravlich's *the beautiful history*.

I saw the town through the eyes of an adventurous young boy, through the stories my parents and grandfathers told, as well as those of my extended family of 25.

Jobs were plentiful and well-paying in these years. There was confidence about the future, and if a man worked for the mines, he could take out a subsidised home loan from the mining companies. This prosperity meant young couples could stay in Broken Hill, buy a car, have an annual vacation 'away', and raise a family on one income.

This 20-year period was very different to the early days of the town, the years of the Great Depression and World War II, and even the postwar recovery years. And different again after the seventies and eighties when mine life was coming to an inevitable end, at least in terms of large-scale underground mining operations. In 1982–83 ore production was still at levels achieved in 1969–70, but there were 43 per cent fewer employees because of improvements in mining technology.

PEAK PROSPERITY

Broken Hill had a population of 30,000 in 1950 and four mines were in full operation. In 1952 the town had its greatest population of almost 33,000. The town had nearly full employment and high wages compared to the rest of Australia. In 1952 employment on the mines peaked at 6459 employees.[1] Lead bonuses paid to mine workers reached their maximum in 1952 at roughly $40,000 per mine employee in current dollars.

Miners had the shortest working week of any Australian workers at 35 hours as well as annual holidays. It's no surprise that car ownership in Broken Hill reached the highest levels in Australia in the early 1950s.[2] Home appliances like refrigerators, washing machines and air conditioners were commonplace, often bought at a discount from the mines amenities scheme.

PEAK PRODUCTIVITY AND SAFETY

The mines also achieved peak productivity growth of 5 per cent per annum in the magic years. The productivity growth rate in Australia at that time was roughly half that number.[3] Some of the gains reflect changes in mining methods while the rest can be attributed to management practices including contract mining and mine planning.

Mining without a fatality was recorded in 1952 for the first time in the line of lode's history. This was an important milestone. It gave credence to mine managers' views that safety didn't have to be compromised to achieve ore production goals.

THE WOOL BOOM

The pastoral industry of the West Darling also reached its peak in 1950 and 1951 as a result of the Korean War. Wool prices achieved record levels during this war, before falling for the next two decades. This was a brief but extraordinary time for West Darling graziers. It allowed them to invest in their properties, to build dams and woolsheds, and to purchase new farm equipment. It was also a time to bank large cheques to be ready for the inevitable drought and hard times to come. The pastoralists' wealth was spread throughout the town when they came in to shop.

PEAK INFLUENCE

Broken Hill had considerable influence in New South Wales in this period, the likes of which the town wouldn't see again. Unions, companies and council all exerted their power.

The union influence was especially apparent: pubs had flexible opening hours and prices of everything from beer to haircuts were vetted by the BIC, as were movie ticket prices. The BIC even had its own Price Committee.

For the four mining companies, Broken Hill was their 'cash cow'. Achieving high levels of uninterrupted production was an expectation of the Collins Street and London directors. This was the period when Broken Hill funded much of Australia's minerals and industrial company growth.

Besides providing dividends and cash flow for new mine operations like the Pilbara, the city became an exporter of talent. It seemed the Broken Hill mining diaspora spread across the nation. In the mid-1960s there would be an announcement every month or so that a mine manager or commercial manager was relocating to Melbourne or a newly opened mine site.

MAJOR INFRASTRUCTURE

Having a reliable water supply had been an issue for the town from its beginning.

In 1888 an effigy of Francis Abigail, the New South Wales Minister for Mines, was burned as protest against him denying residents use of a government tank called the 'Rathole'. Drought years followed with great frequency, from the Federation Drought to droughts in the late 1940s.

An assured water supply was desperately needed for the mines and the town. The council and the mining companies jointly lobbied the New South Wales State Government to build a water pipeline to the town from the Barka Darling River at Menindee. The pipeline opened in 1952. Eight years later the council also supported the Menindee Lakes Scheme, which provided Broken Hill with assured water for decades to come.

PEAK COMMUNITY

Voluntary organisations thrived at this time, making for an incredible sense of community. The factors supporting community engagement in voluntary organisations were all there: economic security, ample time for pursuing interests outside work, isolation that kept you in the town, and the fact that television didn't arrive until the mid sixties.

As I was researching and writing about the town's deep community engagement, I could hear the voices of my mother and father saying, 'We were in a position to help our community and did so by volunteering our time and skills.' For example, membership in the Country Women's Association in Broken Hill peaked in 1955 at 308. By 1970, membership had fallen to 145, reflecting that mine prosperity was beginning to fall.

The mining companies played an unprecedented role in making community investments, ranging from housing co-operatives to funding parks and sporting facilities, even holiday camps like the Zinc Corp camp at Largs Bay in South Australia.

RECOGNITION OF WOMEN

Broken Hill was regarded as a 'man's town' according to author Jenny Camilleri.[4] You can see why she felt this way. *A Broken Hill Who's Who* was published in 1958. The montage of the 22 people who make up the *Who's Who* were all men. There's not one woman to be seen in the publication. It nominates the RSL Secretary Manager, the Broken Hill Bowling Club President, the Broken Hill Club President, the Show Society President, the Silver City Festival Organiser and the Legacy Club Chairman among the 22 men. These were all important civic institutions in Broken Hill at the time. To my surprise the list doesn't include the mine managers or BIC president or key union figures. Not surprisingly, it points to power and influence being held solely by men.

Women, however, were starting to make their presence felt in important ways at this time. The first woman to hold elected office in Broken Hill was Nydia Edes, a feminist fighting for equal pay who formed the Women's Auxiliary of the Australian Labor Party in Broken Hill.[5] In 1962 she was elected to the City Council, the first woman Alderman. She held office as an Alderman for 12 years. She was a board member of the Broken Hill and District Hospital for 30 years, and was influential through her membership of a raft of organisations from the Country Women's Association and Red Cross to the Women's Justices Association and the Anglican Mothers Club. Nydia was awarded the Queen's Silver Jubilee Medal in 1977.

Women began to be recognised for their community contributions in the 1950s and 1960s, on a par with men. Sister Myra Blanche from the hospital received the Queen's Medal. Numerous other women received an MBE for their service, including Mabel Peoples for her service to social and charitable causes, Doris Taylor for starting Meals on Wheels, Phyllis Gibb from School of the Air and Veronica Crowe for her service to the Country Women's Association. Jean Abbott was awarded an OBE for her service as District Commissioner of the Girl Guides.[6]

Broken Hill women recognised through honours were only a small fraction of the volunteers who served community organisations. They were key to the social fabric of the town. Paid employment was denied to them so they sought out other ways to contribute to the Broken Hill community.

Peak prosperity, peak influence and peak community in the fifties and sixties are defining markers in the city's history. The circumstances and mindsets that contributed to these peaks in the city's long history may have a lot to do with trust and a desire to reach mutually agreeable outcomes. This meant that issues once framed as achieving ore production, or having a safe working environment, were now reframed as achieving production safely. Mine competitiveness could be retained by improving productivity rather than reducing wages, the major cause of the 1892 strike and the 1909 strike. Unions also accepted mechanisation as a means to achieving productivity. Providing for the future with long service leave and holiday entitlements came to be every bit as important to a miner as their pay packet. Investment in an employee went beyond the pay and benefits awarded to include things like dental care and the provision of playing fields. Contributing to a strong community became an objective of the mining companies to advance family and individual welfare.

The magic years came about due to favourable metal and wool prices. But this prosperous time involved more than just being fortunate. It took many years to figure out how different interests could work together, how community could be built and how shareholders and employees could flourish together.

Recasting problems as new solutions – framed in a positive way – is at the heart of modern industrial organisation. It just so happened that Broken Hill in its magic years was in the vanguard of best practice long before it dawned on others.

Chapter 4
The Barka

> Barkandji people and the mussels lived on the Barka for over 45,000 years, it was sustainable.[1]
>
> *Barkindji Elder Badger Bates*

Broken Hill is part of the West Darling region, an area bounded by the Barka, the Indigenous word for river, a life-giving river that fed Indigenous people for millennia. The West Darling covers a massive area that goes north to the Queensland border and west to the South Australian border, accounting for one sixth of New South Wales. Before the miners came the outback graziers, and before the graziers were the First Nations clans – the Wilyakali, the Barkandji/Barkindji, Wanyapariku and Malyangapa.

I didn't know the word 'Barka' in my growing-up years in Broken Hill. We only knew the river as the Darling, named after New South Wales Governor Sir Ralph Darling, when the explorer Captain Charles Sturt chanced upon it in 1829. I first noticed the word 'Barka' in historian Bobbie Hardy's books *West of the Darling* in 1969[2] and *Lament for the Barkindji*,[3] published in 1976. You won't find references to the Wilyakali or Barkindji in Roy Bridges' book, *From Silver to Steel: The Romance of the Broken Hill Proprietary*,[4] published in 1920, nor will you find these Indigenous descriptors in Geoffrey Blainey's seminal work *The Rise of Broken Hill*, published in 1968.[5] Robert Solomon's encyclopaedic work *The Richest Lode: Broken Hill 1883-1988* gives only a fleeting mention of Barkindji land being south of Wilcannia.[6]

For a brief time, from 1913–20, the State electoral district was called Willyama, in recognition of the Wilyakali people of Broken Hill and Silverton. It is ironic that an electoral district was named after First Nations people when it wasn't until 1962 that the *Commonwealth Electoral Act* was passed giving all Indigenous people the right to vote.[7] In the 1888 census of Broken Hill there were 11,288 people of whom only five were counted as Aboriginal.[8]

Electoral districts change with population growth and now the district is called Parkes, extending well beyond the original electoral boundary. It's a mostly semi-arid desert landscape that covers almost 400,000 square kilometres, close to half of New South Wales.

INDIGENOUS LIVES IN PARALLEL TO MINE

In the Broken Hill region in the 1950s and 1960s, I can only remember seeing Indigenous people in the small townships of Silverton, Menindee, Wilcannia and Wentworth. There wasn't an Indigenous kid in my primary school at Alma Public or at Broken Hill High School, nor was there an Indigenous footballer on the teams I played with. If you were in a geography class, as I was, you might have had a field excursion to Mutawintji, or Mootwingee as we called it, 139 kilometres north of Broken Hill and be greeted by an Indigenous ranger. Here Indigenous culture was on full display with rock carvings and cave paintings pointing to a people and rich culture dating back over 5000 years that we knew so little about.

Turning to official statistics doesn't help to better understand the lives of the Indigenous population then or now, even with the six-yearly New South Wales census data for 1954, 1960 and 1966. Nor at school when I was growing up was the feared *Aborigines Protection Act* discussed, the Act which permitted removal of Indigenous children from their families. This Act wasn't abolished until 1969.

THREE STORIES OF INDIGENOUS PEOPLE

I knew of few stories of Indigenous people around Broken Hill in these years. But three that I have come to know about more recently are those of Elder Beryl Carmichael of Menindee who is

Ngiyampaa (relocated from the Carowra Tank mission in 1933), Badger Bates, a Barkindji Elder born on the Barka Darling at Wilcannia, and Ron Riley, a Barkindji/Malyangapa man.

ELDER BERYL CARMICHAEL

Beryl Carmichael was a remarkable Indigenous educator and leader who died on 21 May 2024, at the age of 88. She told her story on ABC Local Radio in 2004 to my high school classmate Peter Jinks. As a tribute to Beryl, a recording of the 2004 interview was replayed on ABC Local Radio on 29 May 2024, eight days after her death. Beryl was educated at the Menindee Mission until it closed in 1949 and then was taught by correspondence by her mother.

When I began kindergarten in 1951, not long after the closure of the Menindee Mission, Beryl's family were told that to retain government support they had to relocate some 483 kilometres east to Lake Cargelligo, far beyond their own country, to Wiradjuri country. There were 12 children in the family. Her parents elected to stay in Menindee without government benefits. The family first lived in a brush hut, then a tent and finally a house in Menindee. They supplemented their father's wages, which he received for working on a sheep station, by trapping rabbits to sell to butchers, hunting animals and catching fish and yabbies from the Barka Darling. As young teenagers, Beryl and her sister also began working as domestics on sheep stations. At 18 Beryl married and went on to have 10 children. Like her mother, she taught her own children by correspondence.

In 1967 she approached the principal of Menindee Central School with a proposal to teach cultural heritage to the students, learned from her family and Elders who had been at the mission. She ran a program at Menindee Central School which continues to this day with Indigenous support staff. According to *The Australian Women's Register*, 'Beryl's lessons in Aboriginal culture and respect were extremely effective and she continued her work in schools for forty years.'[9] She also wrote children's books.

Beryl's influence continues today in the aspirations of Indigenous students at Menindee Central School. A relative of Beryl is Fiona Kelly, now the school principal at Menindee. The small school of 80 is 75 per cent Indigenous. Like Aunty Beryl, Fiona speaks with great pride about her students and their determination to stay in school. Almost all the students at Menindee now complete Year 10 and more are going on to complete Years 11 and 12 and are undertaking post school education. It is a remarkable remote school and a credit to Fiona Kelly and her team. It is a positive story we need to hear and so much of its success is due to the early work of Beryl and the deep understanding Fiona and her staff bring to their teaching.

Beryl took on other roles in later years. In 1982 she began working with the Aboriginal Education Consultative Group and later helped start the Western Aboriginal Legal Service to liaise between the police and the community. She is recognised widely for her contributions to the lives of Indigenous people in the West Darling region.

BADGER BATES

William Brian Bates, or Badger as he is known, is a Barkindji Elder, artist, printmaker, carver and sculptor. Badger is also an educator and a prominent Barka Darling River health campaigner. Badger was born in 1947 at Wilcannia. His mother Emily was born at Cuthero Station on the Great Anabranch of the Barka Darling River in about 1925, where her family lived and worked as station hands. As young boys my brother Ian and I visited Cuthero with family friends from nearby Woolcunda Station. We would catch yabbies 'by the sugarbag full', and have close encounters with goannas and kangaroos.

Badger's description of his time growing up is very different to mine, which was happening just 200 kilometres away. I was living comfortably in a house and going to school in Broken Hill while Badger was escaping the so-called 'Protector'. He described his early life this way:

> I travelled a lot up and down the river with my granny and grandfather when I was growing up, mostly so I wouldn't be taken away by welfare and become one of the Stolen Generation ... Granny used to teach me how to carve emu eggs, boomerangs and other artefacts.

> When I was a kid we didn't have much money. The Barka fed us. It was like a supermarket, we ate yabbies, shrimps, fish and turtles. The old river red gum trees had grubs in the roots, the landscape was our food source.[10]

Badger's artistic body of work is well recognised in Australia and has led to many commissions. His rendering of the formation of the line of lode from a Barkindji dreamtime perspective is shown in the Albert Kersten Mining and Minerals Museum in Broken Hill. He was one of a dozen sculptors who in 1993 created the sculpture park outside of Broken Hill called Living Desert Sculptures, a major tourist attraction. In 2023 the Australian Museum in Sydney had an exhibition called *Barka: The Forgotten River*, developed by Badger Bates, Justine Miller and the Barkindji community. What stood out for me were Badger's linocuts of the Menindee fish kills – kills that led to over one million fish dying, mainly Murray Cod, Silver Perch and Golden Perch. The artwork showing fish skeletons is a moving testimony to how mismanagement has impacted the river. Another commission of his forms the spectacular entrance to the Paul Ramsay Foundation in Liverpool Street, Sydney.

RON RILEY

Ron Riley, a Barkindji/Malyangapa man, was a pioneer. He was employed as a miner in Broken Hill in the 1960s. The *Barrier Miner* newspaper in 1971 shows a photo of Ron handling a loader 3000 feet underground. The article describes him in this way:

> Ron Riley is a man suited ideally for his position. He's no Charles Perkins with a university degree, but he is a well-educated man, brought up in the hard school.

Ron also tells the journalist that he wanted to see more effort to attract Aboriginal men from Wilcannia to work in the Broken Hill mines. He noted that while there were jobs available, there wasn't enough housing for them.

Sarah Martin, an archaeologist and historian, and also Badger Bates's wife, notes that social housing for Indigenous people became available in the 1970s and eighties in Broken Hill. This attracted Indigenous workers to the town and opened up prospects to gain employment in the mines.[11]

Opportunities for Indigenous men in the mines came very late in the history of the line of lode. When Joe Keenan, Barrier Industrial Council President, was interviewed in 1970 for Yorkshire Television, he proudly stated that the mines had hired '... several of our own aborigines in the past two years'.[12]

WHEN THE RIVERS RAN FREE

The Barka Darling and the Great Anabranch of the Darling River cover a large amount of the massive land area of the West Darling region. They part at Menindee, south-east of Broken

Hill, and then rejoin 200 kilometres away near Wentworth. The Great Anabranch, or as we called it the Anabranch, is 480 kilometres long, making it one of Australia's top 20 rivers in length.

An anabranch of a river is often called the ancient river – the original course of the river. As well, an anabranch is often termed an 'ephemeral river', meaning it only flows periodically, when the main channel is in flood. According to Maxine Withers, who wrote *Bushmen of the Great Anabranch*, the Great Anabranch was created about 10,000 years ago when the Barka Darling cut a new course to the east, leaving the old channel to run only when the river was in flood. Maxine's book is the best resource available on the history of the Great Anabranch.[13]

In 1956 the Barka Darling flooded at Menindee and along the Anabranch. My family travelled to Menindee to see the flood, with hundreds of watermelons from gardens and debris rushing by. It was a flood the likes of which we haven't seen since. At the flood height the Barka Darling was a staggering 112 kilometres wide. Graziers remember using their Massey Ferguson tractors to build high levee banks around the town of Wentworth to hold back the floodwaters.

The numerous lakes of the Anabranch also filled but the waters stopped before flooding Woolcunda Station. Nearby Popiltah Lake began to fill, one of the largest lakes of the Anabranch that covers 8000 hectares. I still remember a sense of awe as the water made its way through the vast dry landscape, knowing little could impede its path. The country would thrive once again with the water's passing, as it had done for millennia.

By the time the Menindee Lakes Scheme came into operation in the 1960s you could no longer say the rivers ran free. The Anabranch was given an annual replenishment flow of 50,000 megalitres each year from Lake Cawndilla, near Menindee. However, the presence of 17 block banks and weirs meant weir pools held water back from flowing to the Murray. Despite the replenishment flow, the Anabranch was deteriorating with increased sedimentation, salinity and blue green algae in the weir pools.[14] This mighty and ancient river system was, in the space of a few decades, about to run dry.

WHEN THE RIVERS RAN DRY

The Menindee fish kills of December 2018 and January 2019 awakened us all to the state of the Barka or Lower Darling. As well as Murray Cod and Silver and Golden Perch, Bony Herring and Carp also died in huge numbers. The cause, according to the Murray Darling Basin Commission, was high temperatures followed by a temperature drop impacting dissolved oxygen levels. The lack of flow was due to low rainfall, evaporation rates and an over allocation of water in the Basin.[15]

Much has been said and written about how we got to this point. If we look at the condition of the river in 1950, we had river flow and an absence of flow regulation.[16] From about

1950 a series of changes in flow regulation and flow occurred that have brought us to the present situation of the Barka Darling. Water from the pipeline from Menindee to Broken Hill arrived in 1952. This project was widely applauded in Broken Hill bar a few dissenters. Most of all it brought water security to Broken Hill. It was estimated that '… the water needed to support Broken Hill represented less than 1% of the Darling's average flow'.[17] Fifty years later the water supply from the Barka Darling was no longer enough to meet the town's needs. A new 270-kilometre pipeline was built from Broken Hill to Wentworth to tap the Murray River and ensure Broken Hill's water supply. The cost was estimated at $500 million.

The fate suffered by the Anabranch is even worse than that of the Barka Darling. The Anabranch only fills when the Barka Darling is high at 6 metres with flow at 10,000 ML/day.

In 1980 the New South Wales Government proposed 'a scheme to replace the flows in the Anabranch with a six-inch pipeline'.[18] Anabranch residents were opposed to the proposal, because in their view it would destroy the natural system. When New South Wales Premier Neville Wran visited the Anabranch, grazier Peter Crozier of Tor Downs Station had a message for the Premier: 'Tell Mr Wran that he won't get yabbies out of a pipeline.'[19]

In 2007 the New South Wales State Government constructed a water pipeline on the Anabranch, removed many of the weirs, block banks and structures, and provided environment flow every two to three years. By 2016 the New South Wales Parliament was advised by Anabranch Water, the implementing agency, that there were ecological benefits from the return to an ephemeral system. Fish species had increased from six to 13 from 2002 to 2010–12. Fish are now able to move from the Murray to Menindee. On the other hand, businesses were impacted by a less permanent system with periods of low or no flow.[20]

AND THEN THERE'S CLIMATE CHANGE

What was suspected but couldn't be proven is that climate change helps explain the low flows in the Barka Darling in recent decades. Former Broken Hill High School student Lance Leslie, now Professor Leslie, is a climate scientist who has recently published findings that global warming–induced atmospheric circulation changes are even more important than over allocation and diversion of water in the Darling River.[21] Lance and a colleague concluded that since 1992 statistically significant declines in average rainfall have occurred in the all-important March to May period – for this is the time of year when rainfall is needed in the catchment to restore river height.

THE FIGHT GOES ON

The fish kills on the Barka Darling in recent years have drawn the attention of politicians and water officials to the plight of the river. Coalitions of interested parties have formed to highlight concerns of locals and to get water policy change. Badger Bates campaigned with the Darling River Action Group as a cultural advisor. The Action Group was led by my South Broken Hill schoolfriend Ross Leddra, who died in 2025. Ross was a resident of Copi Hollow, part of Menindee Lakes. Ross brought deep local knowledge of the lower Darling system and the directness of someone raised in Broken Hill. He wasn't afraid to criticise water management policy and decisions taken on flows that were in error. For the first time in a long time, in May 2024, he was more optimistic about the future. He saw more politicians and irrigator groups listening and engaging with local views on managing the river, particularly in achieving better water flow. Listening precedes policy change, was his hope.

For Badger, and many others, it's a battle that they keep fighting and won't give up on. They remain hopeful that policymakers will prioritise the health of the Barka Darling, and that policy will be built on careful listening and an acceptance of the realities of low flow and over allocation.

There is so little that we know of the Indigenous people of Broken Hill in the 1950s and 1960s. It's only recently that we have come to understand the importance of the Barka Darling to the Barkindji people, their deep cultural respect for the river. It's time to draw on their knowledge of how to look after a river to make it healthy again to support people and nature.

Chapter 5

Grazing at the Margins

> The lean years alternate with the rich ones in inexorable cycles west of the Darling, and more than once before now the land has exacted terrible penalties when the day of reckoning has come around.[1]
>
> *Bobbie Hardy*

Broken Hill writer Bobbie Hardy captured the challenges of grazing in the West Darling with all of the difficulties and variables of drought and stocking numbers. In the early 1950s, with booming wool prices from the Korean War playing out, and good rainfall years allowing for reasonable stocking rates, Australia was seen to be 'riding on the sheep's back'. At school, we knew our local pastoralists were receiving record high wool cheques. Graziers came into town to shop, most with big welcoming smiles and open wallets.

Pastoralists were good clients of Elders, the stock and station agents in town. They were also good clients of tractor and machinery makers. They could afford to send their children to boarding school for their high school years. Others would invest in light aircraft to locate sheep and goats across the many kilometres of their properties, and to herd them into yards to be shorn or to go to market. Graziers could afford to employ station hands and have some leisure time. The fifties and sixties are mostly remembered as good years despite a drought in 1967.[2] Along with the heyday period in Broken Hill's mining, all seemed to be well for the graziers of the West Darling.

DAYS OF RECKONING

What we weren't taught at school was that crises for West Darling graziers had begun half a century earlier. In 1901 the New South Wales Government had to step in to set up the Western Lands Commission – a body still in operation today. As a result of the 1901 Commission, sheep numbers continued to fall to meet the recommended stocking rates. Between 1901 and 2002 sheep numbers fell from 10 million sheep to 3.5 million across the Western Division, the decline bringing with it more sustainable grazing practices.

AUSTRALIA'S FIRST NATURAL RESOURCE MANAGEMENT PLAN

Australia has 54 natural resource management regions, referred to as NRMs. The first region to have a NRM plan in Australia was the Western Division of New South Wales, following the 1901 inquiry. The Western Division includes the West Darling and represents about 40 per cent of New South Wales.

By the 1880s settlers had taken up the land of the Western Division as leases of Crown land. Blocks along the Barka Darling River and Great Anabranch had been taken up decades before, from 1846. It was only land without water or remote country like the Scotia Blocks, contiguous to the South Australian border, that wasn't settled. The government was trying to avoid having blocks that were too big, closing out opportunities for families, and blocks that were too small for pastoralists to be viable. The problem came to a head in 1900 when tenants of the Western Lands faced ruin.

Drought, overstocking and rabbit infestation were considered equal contributors to the problems graziers faced. Leasing fees and leasing tenure needed to be reviewed. Conservation of land had to be considered. Stocking rates needed to come down from roughly one sheep every 10 acres to one sheep every 20 acres. Closer settlement policies needed to reflect the viability of leases in particular areas. The recommendations relating to rentals, conservation and control over land use were enshrined in the *Western Lands Act of 1901.*

GRAZING ECONOMICS

Sheep grazing in the West Darling sounds like a simple enterprise, but it isn't. You might think there's little more to it than to settle on a sheep breed, set a joining cycle for rams with ewes, monitor your green feed and 90-day weather forecasts to determine stocking, and go buy your rams and ewes. This might allow you to turn a profit if wool prices are high, but if they are depressed and you enter a period of drought, you'll be faced with selling breeding stock into an oversupplied market for lambs and ewes.

There are a myriad of factors that will affect what profits a grazier achieves, including the size of their property, the wool price, the amount sold, the lambing rate and the price of lambs.

The wool yield (kilograms of wool per sheep) is affected by genetics and feed. The amount of feed depends on the seasonal conditions such as the timing and amount of rain. It is also impacted by the total grazing pressure from other herbivores such as goats, kangaroos and rabbits. Rabbit infestations dramatically reduced after CSIRO released the myxomatosis virus in 1950. The rabbits, however, genetically adapted and then in 1995 the CSIRO developed the calicivirus. Scientists will need to continue to develop resistant strains of the control virus.

Lambing rates are affected by changing climate conditions, in particular extreme heat or cold, and the density of sheep who are drinking at a particular watering point. A lot of things have to fall in your favour to have sustained profitability. This semi-arid region is truly grazing at the margins.

WOOLCUNDA STATION STORY

I have a personal vantage point on the pastoral industry of the West Darling, as a long-time friend of the graziers at Woolcunda Station. The property is located between Broken Hill and Wentworth at the end of the Great Anabranch lake system. It is just over an hour's drive from Broken Hill.

It is a story of how five generations of the Anderson/Seekamp pastoralists sought to operate a sustainable sheep property through good times and bad. I have seen first-hand the fortunes, the resilience and how this family managed personal tragedy.

George Anderson took up his Western Lands lease in 1918. He was the first of the five generations to live on Woolcunda. George's granddaughter Hilary married Carl Seekamp and they became the leaseholders of the sheep station.

From the time my family first bought a car in the early 1950s we were regular visitors to Woolcunda Station. It was a typical size West Darling property at a little over 100,000 acres (43,000 hectares). Woolcunda was at the far end of the Great Anabranch overflow, with Woolcunda Lake a major feature when full. The ancient lakebeds were well defined and host to hardy native vegetation like saltbush and bluebush. There was also sandhill country that hosted spinifex and more than a few reptiles.

Carl's knowledge of the seasons and the land's carrying capacity led him to a conservative management regime. He stocked at levels at or below the Western Lands lease requirements. He had built in a margin of safety in his stocking rates. His conservative management meant that he had no time for stations that were 'flogging the land' as he put it. He believed this wasn't the Anderson/Seekamp way to manage Woolcunda.

On our visits to Woolcunda, Carl would take my brother Ian, my father and myself around the 400 square kilometre property. Carl checked paddocks to assess the flock's condition and monitor any lamb losses. He stopped at dams to check water levels and that water from bores was flowing. When I asked why enormous paddocks were empty of sheep, Carl would explain that he was resting the land. This eventually came to be called rotational grazing and adopted as best practice. Only a few sheep station managers were using rotational grazing even by the late 1960s. He enjoyed shocking his young town visitors, my brother and I, when he would whistle like an emu chick to attract a mother emu. As Carl whistled, the mother would run alongside his utility vehicle, searching for a 'missing' chick, even bending her neck to look inside the window.

There was strong social cohesion among neighbouring graziers, isolated from the towns north and south of these large properties. Neighbours would pitch in to help one another with big jobs like bore pipe replacement and fighting bushfires.

Conversation among these graziers inevitably turned to the long-range weather forecasts, in particular those of the very popular Inigo Jones and his assistant Lennox Walker. Their long-range forecasts, when accurate, could help graziers with decisions to take on more sheep or move them off before conditions deteriorated and prices fell.

Shortly before he died, Carl Seekamp handed management of Woolcunda to his son Rob in 1993. Rob had served his apprenticeship with his dad for over 20 years. Rob Seekamp saw good times and difficult times in running Woolcunda. Wool prices had a steady rise from 1970 to 1990 and then dropped dramatically when the Reserve Price Scheme for wool collapsed. As well, the region went into drought for five years. Woolcunda and nearby stations were given the classification 'exceptional circumstances', thereby qualifying for drought relief funding.

Angus Seekamp joined his father, Rob Seekamp, in managing Woolcunda after earning his degree from Charles Sturt University and gaining experience working at a bank in rural finance. Rob and Angus took several decisions about running Woolcunda to improve profitability. In 2008 they decided to run Dorpers, a sheep breed that doesn't grow wool but is sold for meat value. They turned the herding and sale of goats into a large-scale venture to supplement sheep meat income. Rob was able to take advantage of his ability to use his Cessna 172 for rounding up the goats for transport.

Rob Seekamp died tragically at age 57 in 2010 when his plane plunged into Woolcunda Lake on his own property. Rob was an experienced pilot having flown for 40 years. On his way to a meeting in town, he would have been taking in the rare sight of Woolcunda Lake filled for only the fifth time in 100 years. Rob was much loved in the West Darling for the leadership roles he played with the Isolated Parents and Teachers Association, Agfair Broken Hill, and as President of the Pastoralists Association of the West Darling (PAWD). The memorial service for Rob at the Civic Centre in Broken Hill was packed full to honour this well-regarded steward of the land.

Vic Seekamp, Rob's wife, and their son Angus bought Warwick Station, a 45,000-acre property south of Woolcunda, which gave them more acreage and permanent water from the Great Anabranch. Angus bought a truck for transporting stock, a cost-saving measure and a revenue stream to augment what the grazing and herding activities yield. Angus and his wife Chelsee have their own house on Woolcunda now, the fifth generation to live at the station. However, Warwick Station was recently taken over by RZ Resources to mine for mineral sands. Mining takes precedence over other land use throughout Australia regardless of whether the property is leased or is freehold. This possibility was a big concern for Rob Seekamp in his lifetime, and he raised this issue with other graziers at the Pastoralists Association of the West Darling.

Each year at Christmas time Vic Seekamp writes a Woolcunda Update. The Update for 2024 had a familiar ring to it:

> Some good one-off rains, but not enough to fill dams, and the rain's bad timing, with no follow up, has meant not much grass in the paddocks. A dry Spring saw a huge number of ants invade our garden.

As always, grazing at the margins continues at Woolcunda.

For the centenary anniversary of being on the land, in 2017 the Seekamp family self-published a book, *Woolcunda Station: A Century of Shepherding*. I was invited to write the Foreword to the book, having known the four generations of stewards of the land. I wrote that, 'Throughout their stewardship of the land they have kept the next generation uppermost in their minds.'[3] They have consistently managed the property for the long term, not the short, despite the changing environment for shepherding.

THE NEXT CENTURY OF WESTERN LANDS

Regenerating the land that Bobbie Hardy wrote about over 50 years ago is still taking place.

The challenge of grazing at the margins remains. One solution is to diversify sources of income as we saw at Woolcunda. Another example is Belmont Station near Silverton, a property I used to visit. Today Belmont has grazing, a wind farm and is the venue for the Mundi Mundi Bash, an event held each year that attracts over 10,000 visitors.

As climate change continues to make arid grazing more difficult, it is opening up new opportunities for how the resilient graziers of the West Darling use their land. If carbon and biodiversity markets develop, the land will increase in value. There is also the broader potential of renewable energy projects like solar and wind, which could become new sources of income for graziers. In all likelihood, we will see more diversification of land use to make ends meet on the Western Lands.

For over a century, change has been a constant for graziers in the West Darling and this looks to continue. Graziers such as the Seekamps exemplify the challenge of maintaining a sustainable operation as markets, weather and climate all change.

Chapter 6

Miners and Conservationists Join Forces

> There was practically no vegetation ... and the mountain of tailings blew into every crack, corner, dish and bed with every wisp of wind.[1]
>
> *Herbert Hoover*

These were the words of Herbert Hoover in 1905, then a mining investor when he made his first trip to Broken Hill and who later became the 31st President of the United States. He thought it one of the 'dreariest places' he'd ever seen. A half a century earlier, the explorer Captain Charles Sturt noted a very different landscape, when he described the Barrier Ranges as covered in thick native vegetation. This was during Sturt's Central Australia expedition of 1844. The photographer and painter George Jenkinson painted the line of lode in 1888 and featured native vegetation in the foreground. But by 1905 the landscape had been denuded by tree clearing, mining and smelting operations, as well as by house building, drought, overgrazing and rabbit plagues. One resident, Ina Pearl Delattore, born in 1891, gives an indication of the scale of the problem:

> People understood tree-clearing was making the dust worse, but the entire town ran on wood ... My first memory is nothing but horse teams and more bullock teams all day long carting wood, because everything was fired with wood. The pumping station, the mines, the bakers – everything.[2]

Over many decades the natural environment had taken a pounding and this presented the town of Broken Hill with an enormous challenge.

ALBERT AND MARGARET MORRIS'S REGENERATION VISION

The vision to plant a significant fenced-off buffer of native vegetation around the town to stop sand drifts was that of botanist Albert Morris and his wife Margaret. It took many years to achieve but when it was completed in 1958, it was considered one of the most important projects undertaken by conservationists and miners. With these two parties working in partnership, the 'regeneration area' as it came to be known, safeguarded the mining site operations, addressed a serious environmental problem, and improved life for the community.

Early pictures of the Morrises' house show sand banked up around their property. After the regeneration area was completed, people no longer had to stay indoors during sand storms, their doors and windows closed. The native vegetation surrounding the town effectively stopped the heavy drifts of blowing sand, containing it within the fenced-off perimeter. It was the first project of its kind in Australia.

REALISING THE VISION

As well as the years of work by the Morrises and other field naturalists, the leadership and commitment of W.S. Robinson was instrumental to the realisation of their vision of a ring of vegetation to stop sand drifting.

Robinson was the managing director of the newly opened mine, New Broken Hill Consolidated. To protect the new plant, Robinson knew he had to find a way to keep out the destructive sand. He asked his mine manager, A.J. Keast, what could be done. Keast in turn sought the advice of Maurie Mawby, who was the mill manager at the Zinc Corporation which had been mining the area for three decades. This chain of events led Mawby to introduce Albert Morris to Robinson at New Broken Hill Consolidated.

A self-taught botanist, Morris was working as the technical manager at the Central Mine, which had been operating since the 1880s. Morris was also the secretary of the Barrier Field Naturalists Club which he and his wife began in 1921. They were supported by over a hundred other enthusiastic naturalists in Broken Hill. This was a very large number of members for a small town. They identified desert flora specimens from all over the district. They collected seeds and propagated them in their nursery. Importantly, they knew that the natural state of the countryside hadn't been a desert at all and had a good sense of how the denuded land around Broken Hill could be regenerated. Margaret Morris captures this optimism in a *Journal of Science* article in 1939:

> Before the advent of the white man about 1860, the country was thickly covered with scrub of various sorts, the hilly ground supporting typical 'mulga shrub' (*Acacia aneura*), which formed the dominant tree, in association with mallees.[3]

Morris's vision of a buffer of suitable vegetation came about somewhat accidentally, in what I would call a 'natural experiment'. The experiment took place at the town of Cockburn on the South Australian border, some 50 kilometres from Broken Hill. In 1921 Morris visited the railway enclosure in Cockburn – an enclosure built to keep out rabbits, goats and stock. Inside the enclosure plants were thriving but outside was another matter altogether. Vegetation was sparse, eaten away by stock and feral animals.[4] Earlier, fellow field naturalist Dr William McGillivray had observed a similar experiment at the South Racecourse enclosure in Broken Hill where stock had also been fenced out.[5]

The railway enclosure experiment that Morris observed served as a control to contrast with the unmanaged environment around it. Morris was able to see that fencing was a necessary requirement of any successful revegetation effort. The Morrises also experimented at their home to determine which native vegetation would bind with sand and control sand drifts, such as the ever hardy saltbush. Morris could also see that revegetation needed to be undertaken at scale, which led to the eventual concept of a green belt buffer 14.5 kilometres long and 800 metres wide, almost 12 square kilometres. This is an area 4.2 times the size of today's Sydney CBD. Morris had long had the vision but lacked the resources to implement the work until the mines, Broken Hill Council and the community also embraced the concept.

The 're-gen', as we called it, began at the edge of town, at the end of the street where I grew up, Bonanza Street in South Broken Hill. As young boys my brother Ian and I couldn't resist climbing over the fence into the restricted area. My father talked frequently about the history of the regeneration area and the miners and naturalists who made it happen. It was a local history story he was very proud of.

Writer Horace Webber, in his book *The Greening of the Hill*,[6] and Peter Ardill's much more recent online article,[7] capture many features of the story that go a long way to explaining the success of the project. It is the problem-solving aspects of this remarkable joint undertaking by miners, conservationists and the community that captivate me. The cast of characters and their motivations and passions varied hugely. W.S. Robinson was trying to address a problem facing his business as head of the New Broken Hill Consolidated mine. He wasn't proposing a nature conservation project for the good of the town, but out of this self-interest, he opened the way for Morris's dream of a regeneration buffer to be planted around Broken Hill. They all worked together to solve the problem. Even when the New South Wales Erosion Committee went to the town to hear local concerns back in 1935 and 1936, nothing came of their visit. Sydney University had also been consulted about the regeneration proposal, but the university was very dubious, saying, 'If you enclose x square miles of sand with a rabbit-proof fence you will have what you started with – x square miles of sand.'[8]

The university missed the part about trials to introduce natural vegetation, which would in time continue to produce seed to cover the area.

COMPLETING THE VISION

Trialling natural vegetation species in small fenced-off areas was critical to the long-term success of the regeneration area. The first trial was given the no-nonsense name of 'Plantation 1', a 22-acre area where 1600 river red gums were planted and watered by the mines with water they had carefully conserved for this purpose. As well, they planted 1000 old man saltbush to serve as a barrier. They soon had nine types of grasses growing. It was an early success and allowed the mines, and later the

Broken Hill Council as well as the New South Wales State Government, to enthusiastically embrace the project and financially commit to expanding the regeneration to other areas.

Plantation 1 came to be known as the Zinc Lakes. Fittingly, the entrance to the lakes was named the Albert Morris Memorial Gates, in honour of Albert Morris who died in 1939.

We are not used to hearing of miners and conservationists working together. They did so at Broken Hill over two decades to 1958, completing the entire regeneration area to solve a major problem for mines and the community. The residents were also very involved. When the Barrier Field Naturalists lobbied to enclose the common areas that had long been used for grazing, mushroom foraging and collecting firewood, the residents protested. They had to be convinced that the gains from the regeneration project would outweigh the losses of use of the common. The residents were eventually persuaded to support this plan to achieve regeneration success.

LONG-TERM IMPACTS

Beyond Broken Hill, the success of the regeneration project had flow-on impacts. Maurie Mawby's part in the project was living testimony that miners and conservationists could work together around shared objectives. He later became Chairman of Con Zinc Rio Tinto Australia (CRA) and along with Sir Garfield Barwick became a founding trustee of the Australian Conservation Foundation (ACF) in 1965.

In new mines at Mary Kathleen in the Northern Territory and Weipa in Cape York, managers sought to apply learnings from Broken Hill's regeneration efforts and planning for community amenity. Keast led the project at Mary Kathleen while the work at Weipa was led by Maurie Mawby.[9] However, the environment around these areas was very different from the arid environment of Broken Hill. In 2024 I flew over Comalco's rehabilitation efforts after strip mining of bauxite around Weipa. I agree with ecologists' assessments that effective rehabilitation is a big challenge, and that '... the post-mining landscape has radically different soil and hydrological features compared to the pre-mining conditions'.[10] I take this to mean the results of rehabilitation have not been successful. Comalco are continuing their efforts to rehabilitate this post-mining land.

After the success of the regeneration project another illustration of miners and conservationists working together was the creation of Kinchega National Park in Broken Hill in 1967. The over 44,000 hectare Kinchega sheep station was acquired by New South Wales National Parks with the help of the North Broken Hill mining company and CRA. Kinchega is near the Menindee Lakes and fronts the Barka Darling. It is an important place for bird life. What was unusual was a mine's involvement in creating a National Park – an acquisition that was both philanthropic and community related – and predated by several decades more recent corporate acquisitions for conservation.

As I researched the history of the Broken Hill regeneration project, I wondered if anything was missing from this remarkable model of collaboration between miners and conservationists. What comes to mind half a century later is that mine life completion agreements hadn't been put in place. These agreements, now common, detail how land impact is to be addressed by a mine, through revegetation or other means, and they also include plans for income generation when the mine closes. Today's mine life completion agreements spell out actions to ensure that air, land and water won't become a continuing source of environmental or health risk.

Broken Hill's regeneration area was a first in Australia and probably in the world. It was written about and widely talked about. Nature could fight back as pressures were removed. However, a quarter of a century ago I used the word 'fragile' to describe the Gondwana Link in Western Australia between the Fitzgerald and Stirling Ranges, Australia's only terrestrial biodiversity 'hot spot'. Conservationist Keith Bradby said to me, 'No, Rob, this is a resilient landscape that is as tough as an old boot. It might look in bad shape now but with the right care and protection it bounces back.' Just as it did on the perimeter of Broken Hill as Albert Morris envisioned.

The regeneration area in Broken Hill is a remarkable case of problem-solving, with careful evaluation of choices and sufficient experiments and trials that could then be replicated to take the project to scale. The role of local people, Albert and Margaret Morris and their naturalist volunteers who had expertise in native vegetation, can't be overstated. With mine leadership, it was a model of miners, community and conservationists working together for common goals.

Chapter 7

Mining a World-Class Orebody

I have in my hand a 2.04 kg piece of galena, 100 mm in diameter. It was mined in the 1950s, some 900 metres underground on the 18th level of Zinc Corporation. It's a gift I received from my Uncle Alister, a shift boss and head of safety at Zinc Corporation. Half the town would have had a similar specimen from the mines. I keep it in my collection of minerals, a reminder of my father and uncle and the heritage that I am a part of. Growing up in a mining town, a common expression for anything surprisingly heavy was, 'It's as heavy as lead.' The galena specimen I'm holding is both heavy and indeed lead, made up of lead sulphide, and silver. Alongside the chunk of galena, I have a glittering piece of sphalerite, which is zinc sulphide. These two specimens represent a world-class orebody with three major revenue streams – silver, lead and zinc.

Two decades of largely uninterrupted production, underpinned by innovation, exceptional productivity growth and good labour–management relations, was a high mark for Broken Hill mining between 1950 and 1970. An often-heard view was that mine management was slack and doing the Barrier Industrial Council's bidding, but the numbers tell a different story with productivity at its heart.[1]

Unions and management negotiated high pay rates and secure jobs while the mines achieved good shareholder returns and remained competitive via rapid productivity growth. This mutual dependence of unions and management – built up from 1925 with the success of collective bargaining – was the backdrop to this positive picture. Each side could declare victory, unlike much earlier times in Broken Hill's mining history, when one side's gain was another's loss.

There is a touch of irony in the fact that so few days were lost to industrial action in Broken Hill in this period, whereas in other parts of Australia industrial action was heating up, most notably with the eight-month strike at Mount Isa in the 1960s. Ongoing unrest and strikes in the New South Wales coalfields were continuing as well. The newspaper stories about the coalfields, published in the Communist Party of Australia's *Common Cause*, seemed a world away from the issues Broken Hill mine management and unions were resolving amicably. This made Broken Hill mining unique, a paragon for industrial agreements.

MINE OPERATIONS IN THESE MAGIC YEARS

Cavernous stopes – long openings to expose orebodies – were created to mine the silver, lead and zinc, teeming with hundreds of miners, rail lines, locomotives and pneumatic-powered heavy equipment. It took on the look of a huge underground amphitheatre. From the Pay Office where I worked at this time, I could see the miners arriving in large numbers and heading to the cage to take them underground. I was in awe of both the miners and the mine manager's ability to undertake such difficult operations safely.

The mining of the orebody was an incredibly complex task, and the operations extremely sophisticated. In the case of the two largest mines, Zinc Corporation and NBHC, it involved deploying large numbers of men underground on multiple levels. Development teams were sent in first to map the orebody, followed by the miners to extract the ore and transport it to the mill to separate it into lead and zinc concentrate.

While the mines were thinking in 10–15-year timeframes and beyond, volatile markets for silver, lead and zinc often forced companies to re-evaluate their plans. I used to think of the years from 1950 to 1970 as one long boom. It felt that way in our family household. In fact, it breaks down into three distinct eras.

BOOM TIMES: 1950–57

The price of lead and zinc soared to record levels during the Korean War, which ended in July 1953. Ore production came close to doubling in this period. Even bigger news was that productivity grew at an extremely rapid pace, almost four times the rate being achieved elsewhere in Australia. In this period there were innovations in blasting, like the introduction of ANFO (Ammonium Nitrate Fuel Oil) to replace gelignite. Increased productivity also came with the shift to more open stope mining. It was also a time when efforts to measure productivity, such as time and motion, were introduced.

The 1953 industrial agreement between the Barrier Industrial Council and the Mine Managers Association focused on entitlements rather than pay or working conditions. This isn't surprising as pay rates were high for union members, augmented with the substantial level of the lead bonus. The agreement included provisions for the observance of Anzac Day as a paid holiday, and two days were added to annual leave in lieu of observing Australia Day and the Queen's Birthday on the days observed by the rest of the State. The long service leave scheme provided for three months' paid leave in respect of each period of 20 years of continuous service in the industry.[2] A 1956 agreement made salary adjustments to miners not working on contract, with classifications of margins above the basic wage. Conditions for earning long service leave were also improved. These changes were a fine-tuning of a framework that was working well for miners and mining companies.

SOME RECESSION YEARS AND BELT TIGHTENING: 1958–63

Although Broken Hill's mining heyday period, 1950–70, brought great prosperity to the town, an unexpected recession arrived in 1958. It was a shock to the town.[3] The lead price fell 20 per cent from the previous year and the zinc price by 25 per cent, although silver prices were largely unaffected. The lead-zinc industry went into recession and remained there for the best part of six years according to former CRA Chief Executive John Ralph.[4]

This recession required a quick management response. It highlighted once again that costs matter in mining. The Broken Hill South mine, the smallest producer, especially felt the squeeze and reported a loss in mining in 1959 before returning to profitability. The other companies traded profitably but their returns were modest, achieving a 7 per cent return on shareholders' funds. The companies responded to lower prices and weak demand by tightening their belts and reducing the mine workforce. Over 1000 jobs were lost on the line of lode in this period, a 25 per cent reduction. Mine production over the five years was effectively flat, but with a much-reduced workforce producing the same ore tonnage, productivity increased dramatically by a staggering 11.5 per cent per annum.

There was also a national credit crisis in the middle of this belt-tightening period, another reminder the town wasn't insulated from the wider world.

Apart from a four-day strike in 1958, it remained a period of industrial harmony. Once again it is hard to argue that the unions achieved gains at the expense of the mining companies in this period given the productivity gains attained.

PROSPERITY WITHOUT PRODUCTIVITY: 1964–70

Lead and zinc prices improved from 1964 onwards as industrial economies rebounded. Silver prices rose considerably as did industrial demand across a range of sectors. The stage was set to raise production and productivity with substantial capital investment in mechanisation and new methods of mining.

What happened to productivity is something of a puzzle. Ore production continued to increase modestly each year, other than at Broken Hill South which was nearing the end of mine life. Unlike the previous periods where employee numbers fell, mine employees increased from 1964 to 1970. The result of miner numbers increasing was that productivity barely improved over the period, little more than 1 per cent per annum. You would have thought that production would have also increased, but that wasn't the case. The focus instead was on how many tons of ore was mined, not the tons per employee. Peter Coates AO, a mining leader, was an Assistant Underground Manager at Zinc Corp from 1965–71. He stated that the focus was on annual production targets and said he never heard the word productivity mentioned at this time. Leigh Clifford, who later became CEO of Rio Tinto, was a summer student from 1965–67 at Zinc/NBHC and he also confirms that the ethos was 'tons, tons, tons'. Vince Gauci, later CEO of Mount Isa Mines, was a trainee mining engineer at Zinc Corp from 1963–68. His view was there was significant scope for more productivity improvements if the right to manage could be asserted.

TWO MEN TO A MACHINE

The picture I have painted is of the mining companies achieving production goals and mine employees enjoying untold prosperity. By the same token there were long and protracted battles over work conditions underground. An example that sticks in my memory are the negotiations between managers and unions over the two-men-to-a-machine rule.

Mine managers sought to remove obstacles to higher productivity from work practices. The two-men-to-a-machine rule was introduced following a Royal Commission in 1902 after two men died underground. At the time, there was a logic to the rule of having the rockdrill managed by one man and the second man spraying water to contain dust. By the 1950s rockdrill machines were redesigned to incorporate the spraying function, and one man could perform both tasks. Yet the unions insisted on retaining two men for this task.

My father, Frank McLean, a Zinc/NBHC manager, had a more cynical take on the practice, that it was more like theatre. His view was:

> In the 40s, 50s and 60s it became almost standard practice to oppose anything management suggested. The [union] attitude was 'we forced them into safety practices, and we are not going to have them taken away'. The much vaunted 'two men to a machine' in the end became a farcical situation and was eventually ignored by the men underground but resurfaced each time the mines agreement came around, almost like a sacred symbol, although both sides knew how ridiculous it had become.[5]

The rule had real consequences for mining operations. In the 1960s Broken Hill South identified a low-grade orebody near the line of lode, called the western mineralisation. The grades on the line of lode were roughly four times higher than for the western mineralisation. Broken Hill South management estimated that mining this orebody could only be economic if the two-men-to-a-machine rule was dropped, and night shift or weekend work introduced. The major miners' union, the Workers Industrial Union of Australia, wasn't prepared to make the concession.

BROKEN HILL'S HOME-GROWN LANGUAGE BELOW THE SURFACE

We grew up knowing there were frequent negotiations between the unions and the Mine Managers Association (MMA). One

MMA participant said the unions and the MMA were the 'bitterest of friends'. Others, like mine manager Frank Espie, spoke of mutual respect between the two groups. Andrew Fairweather, a mine manager of Broken Hill South, was often acknowledged for his humanity and concern for workers and safety.[6] The shared interest was well expressed by Norm Dunleavy, president of the largest union, the Workers Industrial Union of Australia, when he described stoppages as 'irritations on the surface and free from political intrigue'. He also said the stoppages were usually settled satisfactorily after union–management conferences.[7]

At the mine face there were continual minor skirmishes surrounding work arrangements underground. There was a home-grown Broken Hill language that described these skirmishes as they played out in the stopes, shift by shift, and everyone in town understood these phrases.

A darg: a go-slow tactic to impede production.
A plain loafer: someone who slacked off and failed to complete tasks assigned.
A bludger: a harsh description of an extremely plain loafer.
A malingerer: a worker who consistently had excuses for not working.

There were other terms that indicated tension between management and miners, such as the word *seniority* – the term unions used to give longer-serving men preference for jobs rather than the most productive man, which is what management preferred. Another was the word *victimisation*, which was used to describe unreasonable transfers of men to lower paid work. *Time and motion* was a particularly emotional phrase for miners; this was an American work-study measurement – that of time taken for tasks.

FINDING COMMON GROUND

The art of negotiation is to find common ground and advance your aims on that ground. To my surprise the negotiations between the Barrier Industrial Council and the Mine Managers Association were seldom reported on in this way. The lens most often used to report on negotiations was an out-of-date one: what unions got, management lost, and vice versa. The data I analysed, however, shows that in the 1950s and 1960s both sides largely got what they wanted. Both parties found common ground, even if bargaining favoured one or the other at a particular time.

Management wanted a high level of production, a work-force that could carry out mining under hazardous conditions, the absence of industrial action, the ability to make investments in labour-saving equipment, and cost structures that allowed shareholders to earn reasonable returns, given fluctuations in metal prices. A crucial measure of mine management effectiveness lay in the productivity gains achieved. They were truly world class. Take Zinc Corporation as an example. With productivity growing at 5.8 per cent per annum from 1950 to

1967, the Broken Hill mines were able to be profitable when metal prices fell and could lower their production costs per ton. Of course, this doesn't mean there wasn't some slack or things like absenteeism that couldn't be improved upon.

The mines largely achieved these objectives in this heyday period. In 1965 CRA Chairman Maurie Mawby pointed out that the companies needed to '... be patient and, above all, prevent a stoppage, particularly in these times when we need the money so much for other projects'.[8] In effect he was saying don't do anything that might jeopardise our cash cow from providing milk and cream.

Both the mines and unions wanted fair pay and conditions, a safe working environment, a share in the mine's prosperity, employment for Broken Hill men and for the mines to be long lived. Apart from a bruising loss by the unions in 1950 to accept B-groupers, employment went to locals. The lead bonus reached levels that were material to family income. There weren't layoffs or redundancies in this time apart from the strike over B-groupers in 1950 and the proposal for reduced hours per fortnight for a brief period in 1958.

The industrial agreements, set every three years, were considered the 'bible', in the words of Zinc/NBHC counsel Barton Maughan.[9] Everyone in Broken Hill knew of the Barrier Industrial Council President, Shorty O'Neil, often called the 'King of Broken Hill'. Shorty was a unionist who started work at the mines at the age of 14 in 1917. He lived through the bitter long strike years and this convinced him that strikes weren't the way forward.[10]

There was strong commonality of interests between mine managers and the unions. The mining companies had a long-term view for mining the orebody for profitability. Three-year industrial agreements satisfied the interests of shareholders, mine employees, unions and the community. It was a golden age where much wealth was created with the capacity for it to be shared.

Chapter 8

Wealth for Toil

> Broken Hill was one of the worst examples in Australia of how management neglected the conditions in which employees lived and worked.[1]
>
> *W.S. Robinson, Managing Director of The Zinc Corporation*

The mining manager W.S. Robinson was reflecting on the decades before the 1950s in the quote above. He may well have been very surprised to know that Broken Hill mine management went on to become a leading model of what today is called corporate social responsibility. It was an unprecedented community transformation that took place in the years I lived in the town, between 1950 and 1970. But a 1936 decision predated this transformation when the board of the New Broken Hill Consolidated mine at the southern end of the line of lode '... belatedly began to invest in the community as well as the mines'.[2] These small early steps, however, didn't reach their zenith until the period when I was growing up. This level of corporate social responsibility was the first of its kind in Australia, and along with my family and our friends, we were the true beneficiaries of the mines' community investment.

SHARING THE PIE

The mines' contributions to the community were exceptional, both in terms of the number of initiatives and the number of organisations supported. It's hard to identify another remote community where the scope of services a mining company provided were as comprehensive as in Broken Hill. W.S. Robinson described the mining companies' contributions this way:

> All kinds of social services and civic amenities were started and subsidized: employees' sickness funds, co-operative housing schemes, kindergartens, clubs, sports fields, parks and gardens, hospital and dental services. The mining companies helped to finance improvements to many of the existing amenities such as the hospital, schools, water supply, sewerage and power supply.[3]

As a young boy in the 1950s I wasn't really aware of the shared wealth created by the town's mines, but I knew we were a typical mining family. My father's salary was sufficient to buy a new house in South Broken Hill and like many others he bought his first car. Mum and Dad installed air conditioning in the house, replaced the chip hot water heater with a Rheem, bought a washing machine, a Hills Hoist for drying clothes and a record player. A transistor radio allowed my brother and I to listen to test cricket matches in England late at night. A town-operated sewerage system and television were still a decade away from changing our lives, but we knew they were coming.

When we got our first car, we began to feel less isolated. Possibilities of long weekend trips to Adelaide, picnics at The Gorge, a tree-lined dry creek bed outside of town, or a barbecue at Penrose Park near the ghost town of Silverton opened up for us. By 1953 there were 12,000 motor vehicle registrations in Broken Hill. With a population of 32,000 this meant Broken Hill had the highest car registration in Australia and was second only to the State of New York at that time.[4]

EXCEPTIONAL COMMUNITY INVESTMENT

At the time I was too young to see that the Zinc Corporation's contributions to the community were exceptional, although my mother and father did. Our standard of living stood in stark contrast to their young lives in the Depression and the World War II years. My lens was that of a child. As the sons of a Zinc employee father, my brother and I learned to swim at the Zinc Pool. We played cricket on the Zinc/NBHC ovals and along with our younger sister and parents we attended the annual Zinc Lakes picnic day. For summer holidays we'd often go to the Zinc Corp Largs Bay holiday camp in Adelaide at the seaside, along with a thousand other people, all families of Zinc mine employees.

W.S. Robinson and his fellow company directors at North Broken Hill, and to a lesser extent Broken Hill South, weren't utopian socialists. They were intensely practical businessmen. After years of neglect, focusing solely on production and shareholder returns, they decided to widen the lens on their mining operation investments and focus as well on the interests of all stakeholders. They were ahead of their time in corporate social responsibility. Their community investment was unprecedented then and now.

PAY AND CONDITIONS

Miners worked a 35-hour week in five shifts of seven hours. This was the shortest work week in Australia. On top of a basic wage, there were allowances per shift for skilled tradesmen. Management and unions also successfully negotiated contract rates for specific underground mining parties.

Generous annual holiday leave, paid sick leave and long service leave made for an especially attractive total compensation package. A great deal of the negotiation that took place between the Mine Managers Association and the Barrier Industrial Council through the 1950s and 1960s was about these kinds of employee entitlements.[5]

The total compensation package of a mine employee also included what today we think of as fringe benefits. Mine employees had access to amenities schemes for purchasing white goods at attractive prices and housing finance at concessional rates. For instance, North Broken Hill employees were offered housing loans through their co-operative building society at a concessional 2 per cent interest rate.

A WORLD FIRST: A LEAD BONUS FOR MINERS

In addition to the generous employee entitlements, a lead bonus was paid to all mine employees. It varied each month based on the price of lead. When the price of lead went up, the bonus paid greatly increased a miner's wage. Paying a generous lead bonus wasn't the norm in other mining communities in Australia. It set Broken Hill apart, once again, as a town like no other. The *Sydney Morning Herald* described miners' pay in Broken Hill relative to other occupations in this way:

> At one stage the lowliest mine labourer earned more than the Government mine inspector, a highly trained man carrying out very responsible duties. In Broken Hill, to say a man is a miner has somewhat the same implications as saying, in Sydney, that he is a solicitor … the earnings of the lowest paid adult labourer in the mines there at present are about 24 pound a week (a 12-pound basic wage and 12-pound lead bonus). Some contract

> miners, who were paid piece work rates for ore mined, at that time were making 50 pounds a week [equivalent to a salary of $120,000 a year today].[6]

The lead bonus was originally devised by Broken Hill mining company directors in 1925, although the amount set at this time was at a very modest level relative to lead prices. The introduction of the bonus was in response to a request by the Barrier Industrial Council to have a profit share in return for a no strike period.[7]

Years went by with no payments. During the Korean War the price of lead rose to levels that meant the lead bonus payment scheme wasn't sustainable – it didn't bear any relationship to effort, costs or profits. Labor historian John Shields went so far as to say that if anything there was an inverse relationship between the lead bonus and productivity – that is to say, the higher the lead bonus, the lower the productivity level.[8]

The lead bonus scheme also had a major design flaw in being structured as a pre-tax and dividend payment, much like the royalties paid to the New South Wales Government. In order to provide the right incentive, the lead bonus ought to have been an after tax and royalty payment, not unlike dividends received by shareholders. The lead bonus wasn't paid if there were any strikes and it may have provided an incentive to avoid this kind of industrial action.

ROYALTIES, TAXATION AND RATES

The final set of contributions to the community was in the form of royalties, rates and company tax. These were a sore sticking point for the mining companies. Robert Porter, Rio Tinto biographer, didn't mince words when he argued:

> The Broken Hill mines bore an onerous taxation and cost burden. The top rate of the New South Wales royalty was 50 percent. The addition of Commonwealth Government taxation meant that taxation imposts could be as high as 73 percent. In addition, freight rates, as well as water and municipal rates, resulted in a high-cost structure.[9]

The local council levied rates on the mining companies, comprising a general rate and a special rate. This amounted to approximately $6.6 million per annum.[10] A tidy sum for a town of 30,000 to maintain roads, rubbish and sewerage. Besides the rate payments the mines funded electricity generation for the city and deficit funding for the Water Board, the utility providing water to the town. The mining companies paid a much higher price for water than residents and were prepared to fund most of the deficits of the Water Board. The mines felt they were paying the council too much. Their contribution to the rate base peaked in 1967 at 77 per cent. This ridiculously high rate ended in legal action to reduce it in the early 1970s.[11]

The mining companies paid royalties to the New South Wales Government on what were termed 'third renewal leases'.[12] North Broken Hill's profit of 1.5 million pounds in 1963, if attributed all to mining operations, works out to a royalty of about $5.6 million in today's purchasing power. Across the line of lode this would have meant royalties of roughly $20 million per annum today, no small sum to the New South Wales Treasury.

The final slug went to the Commonwealth in company tax payments. In 1950 the corporate tax rate was 30 per cent before rising to 35 per cent in 1951. It ratcheted up every few years so by 1970 it reached 47.5 per cent of net profit.

RETURNS TO SHAREHOLDERS

The final group to consider are the shareholders, made up of individual investors and company owners. The mining companies were profitable throughout this period, except for Broken Hill South's posting of a mining loss in 1958. From the data I was able to find for one of the companies, New Broken Hill Consolidated (NBHC), they provided about a 13 per cent return to shareholders in 1963, and this was a year when it was emerging from a recessed market for lead and zinc.

Zinc Corporation and NBHC were crucial contributors of earnings to parent company CRA. The author Robert Porter explains in his book *Rio Tinto in Australia*: 'In 1963, the Broken Hill operations constituted 30% of CRA's total shareholder funds and generated 80 percent of the company's earnings.'[13] The earnings and cash contributions were needed to fund the huge mine development pipeline that CRA was building with Comalco, Hamersley Iron, Blair Athol Coal and Bougainville Copper.

North Broken Hill and Broken Hill South were part of what was termed the Collins House group in Melbourne. They were active in reinvesting cash from Broken Hill operations in new mining and industrial ventures. Bill Conn, a former head of Potter Partners, pointed out to me how significant the cash flow from Broken Hill was in creating Alcoa in Australia, Associated Pulp and Paper Mills, Metal Manufacturers and the Dutchess phosphate deposit.

THE BEST OF TIMES BEGINS TO WANE

For Broken Hill miners and their families, it was the best of times in these two decades, but by the early 1970s the Broken Hill South mine closed, and we had the sense that the best days were over. The heyday I've described was characterised by long-term thinking, making the pie bigger and providing fair returns to stakeholders, coupled with heavy community investment. The unions and mine managers largely avoided debilitating strikes and pressed for improved conditions around a pay framework that brought huge benefits to the income of mining families.

We may not see wealth sharing like this again. It wasn't seen in Broken Hill before the 1950s, nor did it continue for long after that. The 1970s were tougher for Broken Hill as opportunities and optimism faded along with the mines' depleting reserves. Productivity and cost became the focus of mine management. Negotiations with unions took on a different course as mine life shortened and the balance of power shifted to employers. As the economic engine of mining waned, the town's population shrunk to a much lower level and community investment by the mines was harder to justify.

The four Broken Hill mining companies invested in the community, strengthened its institutions and made life more comfortable in the hot, dry climate of Broken Hill. They invested in mining technology to improve productivity and lengthen mine life, which sustained well-paid jobs. Even Nobel Laureate Milton Friedman, an economist and capitalist, argued that it may well be in a company's long-term interest to provide amenities to a small community.[14]

Together these mining companies wrote a new chapter on corporate social responsibility before we came to know the expression.

Chapter 9

The Sounds of Silence

Mining exacted a big price in lives lost in the Broken Hill mining industry. There have been more than 800 fatalities in and around Broken Hill since mining began in the late 1800s.[1] Each fatality is recognised, the names inscribed in the Miners Memorial that sits atop the line of lode. It is a striking sculpture that overlooks the town, built in 2001 with a Federation Grant from the Commonwealth, and visited by thousands of tourists each year. Walking along the memorial site, you can't help but notice the high fatality rates in the early years of Broken Hill mining, and then how dramatically they declined over time. In the decade 1900 to 1909 there were 178 fatalities (surface and underground) compared to 18 fatalities underground in the 10-year period 1960 to 1969.

Vickie Drosos came to Broken Hill in 1963 from Greece to marry Nick Drosos. When she was interviewed about her life in Broken Hill, which she came to love, she said, 'Nick is working in the mine underground. It's scary and always you worry because it's not very safe. All the women in Broken Hill are scared.'[2] For women like Vickie and thousands of other wives who lived with this fear, it was a daily concern. Safety was always on the minds of those with loved ones working underground.

I distinctly remember a quiet hum in the air from the Zinc mine, a kilometre from our home. It was a noisier hum when our family moved to a house in Rainbow Avenue, located on the mine lease itself. This quiet hum was regularly punctuated by sirens that marked shift changes. But there was one siren that we all feared – the siren that signalled a fatality had occurred. It was followed by an eerie silence throughout the town as the mines shut down and miners were instructed by the unions to take a day off work.

I asked my friend Bill Hardy who lived on the North mine lease how he recalls the fateful sound of a fatality.

> All mines had their own whistles. They sounded at 7 and 8 am, then 3, 4 and 11 pm, then again at 12 am. If a fatality occurred on the North a siren would blast 12 times. That got everyone going. The unions would announce that there would be no work the next day for its members. Our family lived on the North mine lease adjacent to Number One shaft and very close to all the

noise a mine makes. I can remember asking Dad why there were so many whistles on a particular night, and he replied that miners were trapped underground.

In a tight-knit community like Broken Hill a fatality was only a few degrees of separation away. John Semmens' death in 1973, underground at New Broken Hill Consolidated, was one such occurrence. He was known as 'Jarda', a talented footballer who played in all South's football premierships from 1967–70. He was a ruck rover. Jarda was not only a talented footballer but a leader of men. He was struck by a 'fall of ground' – that is, a rockfall. The coronial inquiry returned a verdict of accidental death.[3] Jarda was only 29, married with young children. My cousin Helen Giblett, who attended Jarda's funeral, said it was one of the biggest funerals Broken Hill has ever had.

LEARNING FROM THE 'FATAL LODES'

Stan Goodman's book *The Fatal Lodes* is an encyclopaedic tome of mining deaths in the Broken Hill district starting in 1885.[4] It catalogues the deaths that took place each year, the circumstances, and the results of the magisterial inquiry (later termed a coronial inquiry), with a jury finding on whether the cause of death was accidental or due to negligence on the part of those involved. Having this information readily available was important to learning how to better manage risks and avoid unsafe practices. But it didn't of itself lead to a safe working environment.

Most of the deaths that Stan Goodman describes in *The Fatal Lode* involved rock falls or men falling between stopes. Of the deaths recorded from 1950 to 1970, the largest cause by far was termed a 'fall of ground'. In several instances before a fall of rock, the inquiry references it with the expression 'the ground talking'. This sound was sometimes a precursor to a fall of ground, leading men to quickly evacuate the stope. The second most frequent cause of death was a fall down a chute or what was known as a winze, and a similar number of fatalities resulted from being crushed or jammed by equipment.

Ensuring safe working environments at the mines was a perennial issue. Examples of the concerns were the union's decision to mark a fatality with a day off work, to union concerns about risks contract miners were forced to take to produce ore. The unions were also concerned about hazardous dust during rock drilling. The mining companies responded by introducing machines to keep dust levels down. They initiated safety programs to highlight and manage risks and an incentive bonus scheme for shift bosses was implemented – effectively a higher pay packet when accidents were reduced.

Sadly, there was no magic bullet that did away with accidents and fatalities. But better knowledge of unsafe conditions and unsafe acts brought a steady improvement in safety outcomes. And elevating safety goals to equal the level of production goals played a role in getting better safety outcomes.

FATALITIES IN THE PERIOD 1950–70

The first fatality of the 1950s occurred on 8 February 1950. The union newspaper, the *Barrier Daily Truth*, reported that miner Jack Kumm died in an explosion in a winze and that all union members would stop work for a day.[5] Jack Kumm was an experienced miner of 17 years, married with three daughters and one son.

As the mines were looking to take advantage of boom prices of silver, lead and zinc in the early 1950s, they needed to increase the workforce with new miners who may not have had mining experience. Safety took on even more significance. The risks increased as miners had to go deeper and deeper in the line of lode while operating on multiple levels. Mine managers at this time were also keen to change from traditional timber stope mining to open stope mining. Timber stopes were believed to be safer than open stopes as the timber support helped prevent rockfalls. Productivity was two to three times higher for open stoping. Miners and unions continued to be sceptical of open stopes – what they saw as open cavernous areas of rock face – but slowly accepted the method favoured by the managers. Over two decades from the 1940s to the 1960s ore production per annum doubled and the fatality rate halved. The managers were able to demonstrate that production could be increased without compromising safety. With newer knowledge about rock mechanics, they were better able to identify unsafe working areas. The improved mechanisation of ore loading also reduced back injuries.

Over the period 1950 to 1970 there were on average 2.3 fatalities each year in underground accidents. Encouragingly, during the whole of 1952 there wasn't a single death from mining.[6] There was the death of Ivica Blazevic in June 1952 at the feldspar mine near Cockburn, recorded at the Miners Memorial. Positive trends emerged across individual decades. There were 29 deaths underground in the Broken Hill mines from 1950 to 1959; this figure then dropped in the following decade to 18, a near 40 per cent reduction. The 1960s saw the mining companies increase their commitment to safe work practices. They began sharing statistical analysis and workplace monitoring data and introduced training in the safe use of safety belts and other equipment.[7]

This change of focus to data collection, monitoring systems, and training that highlighted examples of safe and unsafe behaviour contributed to less fatalities. For example, a miner not leaving the 'talking ground' of rock stresses would most likely be classified as an unsafe act in unsafe conditions, and not merely a near miss. Awareness of unsafe acts underground was critical to these improvements. The analysis showed that half the accidents were due to unsafe acts and the other half to unsafe conditions. Given the challenges of unsafe conditions, the managers were able to bring down the number of unsafe acts with a greater focus on training. There was still a long way to go.

HOW DATA IMPROVED SAFETY OUTCOMES

In 1960 the four mines created the Industrial Accident Prevention Committee under the Mine Managers Association. They developed a standard code of accident reporting, and a common, consistent way of classifying accident causes, separating unsafe acts from unsafe conditions. This allowed comparisons to be made for knowledge sharing between the mines. Reductions in accident rates soon followed across the four mines with the largest reductions at North Broken Hill – an accident frequency rate that was reduced by 25 per cent within a few years. It was a great illustration of the sharing and learning that was possible across the line of lode in this period.

KENNETH MCLEAN – AN ACCIDENTAL HERO

One fatal underground incident involved my grandfather, Kenneth McLean. It was different to most other mining fatalities on the line of lode.[8] Four men died on 18 October 1935 between Crystal Lane where the Palace Hotel is located and the BHP lease. They were just 15 metres below the surface and were overcome by noxious gases. The men who died were the Manager of BHP in Broken Hill, Richard Slee, the BHP Chief Engineer Joseph Giffen, Albert Taylor, a shift boss, and Harold Milligan, a young labourer working as a volunteer at the Palace Hotel. The Palace Hotel had a connecting borehole between the hotel cellar to a dam on the BHP site. The blocked borehole caused a stench, and the BHP mine management were notified; the four men entered the passageway to the mine but didn't return.

My father, Frank McLean, picks up the story in his personal memoir. He describes how his father Ken was summoned to the site:

> My father had an intimate knowledge of the pumps and pipework along Crystal Street. When he reached the site, gas was still emerging from the aperture. He was joined by the Mines Inspector, Mr Wilson, and after discussing the situation they decided to enter the tunnel. In those days there was no breathing apparatus so they used wet handkerchiefs to cover their faces. Descending the ladder they found the body of the young man which was taken to the surface. They then waded some 15 feet into the tunnel where they found the bodies of the other men. They were taken to the surface and the aperture sealed. It was then about 10 pm and a crowd of several thousand had crowded into the area.

The rescuers, Douglas Wilson, Inspector of Mines, the District Fire Officer James Johns, and my grandfather, were awarded a Certificate of Merit and the Clarke Silver Medal, the highest award from the Royal Humane Society for their bravery. The New South Wales Premier wrote a letter to my grandfather, dated 2 December 1935, that reads: 'On behalf of the Government of New South Wales, I desire to express our deep appreciation of the courageous endeavour, at the imminent risk of your own life, to rescue the men who unfortunately met their death as a result of the accident.' My grandfather retired from BHP in 1949, living his last 10 years at Whyalla where I was born. He passed the newspaper stories, letter and honours to my father. He never wanted to discuss the fatalities or his heroic role with me when I was a young boy.

DEEP COMMITMENTS TO SAFETY

The unions were deeply committed to ensuring a safe working environment. Even minor injuries were reported in the local paper, the *Barrier Daily Truth*. For example, on 7 February 1950 the *Truth* described an injury sustained by Mr D. Slater: 'D. Slater (Zinc Corp) was treated for a foreign body in an eye before going home.' Every lost time injury such as D. Slater's was reported, adding to awareness in the community about safety.

Barrier Industrial Council President Shorty O'Neil led many negotiations on industrial agreements. Prior to becoming BIC President, he was a Check Inspector of Mines, appointed under the NSW *Mines Inspection Act*. In this role he visited miners at every stope to see that the stopes were safe working places. His powers included being able to order stope closures for safety reasons. As Check Inspector he also attended accident sites to investigate causes and then propose safer practices. Shorty's knowledge of virtually every stope on the line of lode equipped him well for the BIC President role.

The mining companies had a strong safety orientation. Andrew Fairweather was underground manager of Broken Hill South and MMA President from 1949–54. He remarked that, 'Safety of life and limb must be the first consideration, and ... output and cost must stand aside when men's safety is involved.'[9]

My uncle Alister McLean led safety training for Zinc/NBHC when I was a boy, drawing on his experience as a shift boss overseeing mining operations. This was a key role to build safety into the culture. I recall getting instructions from Uncle Al on how to pick up a heavy box, bending my knees to go down to the box and avoiding back strain.

We all knew the mantra that *safety is everybody's business*. It went further than being a slogan at Zinc/NBHC where the Chief Industrial Engineer, Ossie Blau, said, 'The underlying basis of the safety program is that accident prevention is a line responsibility. ... He [the front-line supervisor] is also responsible for the accident performance of his employees, and the statistics of accidents debited to him measure his degree of success.'[10] Management accountability for safety had become a given in Broken Hill mining operations. The companies changed mining practices in line with known and manageable risks. Opportunities to mechanise physical tasks such as ore loading improved productivity and safety. Signs about safety featured prominently on the surface and in the underground change areas and around the cage taking men underground.

Bill Hardy worked at the North mine as an electrician from 1964 to 1976. He tells the story of how he failed to follow procedures in using a Ramset nail gun. The nail entered his thigh. After recovering, Bill was required to give instruction to a group of mine employees on the safe use of a Ramset gun. Learning and sharing the lessons was part of the culture. Bill felt that not only was there a safety culture but it became a competition between the North and Zinc Corp to see who could have a better safety record.

A ZERO FATALITY MINDSET

In the late 1970s a radical view began to emerge about safety that was central to management practice. It came from management thinkers like Tom Peters and Bob Waterman, as outlined in their book *In Search of Excellence*, British researcher Elliott Jaques who worked with CRA, and Japanese automotive companies like Toyota. All emphasised how critical priority setting, measurement and accountability were to achieving breakthrough performance in production, quality and safety. John Ralph of CRA led the group in embracing this thinking. John was born and raised in Broken Hill and became Chief Executive of CRA in 1987. Recently he told me that he saw safety as a 'mechanism for change'. Management and miners had a common interest in working together on safety. It was about production *and* safety, not production *or* safety. This mindset has been taken up by companies in industries around the world, paving the way for a target of zero fatalities.

When I became a company director at CSR in the late 1990s, safety was paramount for the Board and management. Two fatalities occurred in my time on the CSR Board. One involved road work where a contractor was run over. The other occurred when a workman climbed into a machine to free something and the machine started. These fatalities were the first items on the Board agenda. The business unit head who resided in the United States was flown to Sydney to explain to the Board the circumstances that led to the fatality where a contractor was run over. The lessons learned and the practices that needed to change evolved from that meeting. The message was that safety mattered, managers were accountable, and the Board had a critical role to play in ensuring a safe workplace.

Today our expectations are for zero fatalities. Workplace safety practices are aligned to that goal, even in hazardous occupations. For example, Rio Tinto announced in 2023 they achieved zero fatalities at managed operations for 55,000 employees across six continents. Soon after achieving this result four employees died in a plane crash travelling to the Diavik Diamond Mine in the Northwest Territories in Canada.

The sounds of silence continued to be heard several times a year as I was growing up. It was a reminder of the risks that miners underground faced every day. It's a sound that hasn't been erased with time, but it's heard much less frequently than in decades past.

Chapter 10

The Walled City

In an interview with Yorkshire Television in 1970, Joe Keenan made a startling admission when he said '... we can do almost anything in this town'. Joe Keenan was then the President of the Barrier Industrial Council and he likened Broken Hill to a 'walled city' like in the time of the Romans, and went on to say, '... when in Rome do as the Romans do'.[1] His description wouldn't, however, have been startling to the people back in Broken Hill. They knew exactly what he was referring to. It's a chapter in Broken Hill's history that I call 'social engineering'.

SOCIAL ENGINEERING WITH UNINTENDED CONSEQUENCES

The origins of the Barrier Industrial Council's social engineering dated back to the Great Depression years and concerns about rising unemployment. This issue reared its head in the 1930s when the BIC introduced a policy that prevented married women in Broken Hill from working. The idea behind the policy was two-fold: to ensure young *unmarried* women could find jobs when they finished school and stay in the town, and because the BIC held the prevalent view that men were the breadwinners and their mining wages could support a family. There were a few exceptions in cases where a job was deemed 'women's work', like nursing, or where a woman held professional qualifications, but otherwise when a woman married, she had to give up her job within three months. This was also a time when the Commonwealth Public Service restricted married women from working – a policy not changed until 1962.

This patriarchal policy was in place until 1981 when it was challenged by dental assistant Jeanine Whitehair in a case brought before the Equal Opportunity Tribunal. For half a century Broken Hill women were denied a basic right to employment by the BIC policy. The rule was generally accepted, viewed as being in the community interest at a time when the society saw a woman's role as housewife and mother.

The patriarchal policy had unintended consequences. Firstly, it removed exceptional talent from jobs where a woman could be productive. It also encouraged some women to leave Broken Hill to pursue a career. It nudged women into exempt occupations like nursing and teaching, and encouraged other women to become employers or to self-employ to get around the restriction. Broken Hill had 25 per cent more self-employed women in the 1960s than the rest of New South Wales.

BLACK BANS GALORE

Another example of the BIC's social engineering came with the establishment of a Price Committee in 1948 to oversee the prices of beer, milk, bread, rents and cinema tickets. The backdrop to this decision was the high inflation rate in Australia at that time. Australia didn't get a Prices Justification Tribunal until 1973 and that only lasted until 1981 when it was abolished.

In the first half of the twentieth century an early test of the BIC Price Committee was to intervene when hairdressers increased the price of a haircut by 10 per cent. The BIC stepped in and as historian Ross Kearns says, '… hairdressers were persuaded to revert to the original price'.[2] 'Persuaded' was certainly an interesting choice of words!

Over the next few years 'black bans' were placed on movie theatres and hotels if they increased prices to a level that the BIC deemed unreasonable. When a movie theatre or hotel was declared black, union members weren't allowed to patronise the theatre or hotel, or take a job there. When the hotels were declared black for a week, the customers staying at the hotel had to make their own meals.[3]

Bans were extended to charity work in one instance. Each year the Girl Guides held a bob-a-job week, going from house to house, to raise money for the organisation. My mother would nominate a small job that took a half hour for the girls to do and pay them a bob, which was about $1.60 today. This was declared to be 'competitive work' by the BIC and disallowed. At this low rate it's not clear what workers were disadvantaged by the ban!

In the early 1960s a ban was placed on cakes and pastries being brought in from South Australia. The ban only lasted a few days as it met fierce customer opposition and was promptly lifted. Although this ban violated Section 92 of the Australian Constitution – that is, free trade between States – enforcement of this provision didn't take place until 1988.

At much the same time, the retailer Woolworths was issued with a black ban by BIC President Shorty O'Neil for failing to allocate half of its advertising to the union newspaper, the *Barrier Daily Truth*.[4] Woolworths were allocating all of their advertising to the evening newspaper, the Rupert Murdoch owned *Barrier Miner*. Woolworths capitulated by agreeing to place half its advertising with the *Barrier Daily Truth*.

Otto Holten's was a hardware supplies store in South Broken Hill. I went there with my dad from time to time for building supplies. Visiting Otto's was like being in a mid-eastern bazaar with tunnel-like passageways and dirt floors.

We called it a 'rabbit warren'. Otto earned the ire of the BIC for exercising what he thought was a management prerogative. A young girl who was working for him had taken several days off due to illness. It was reported to Otto that she had been seen out shopping when she was supposed to be recovering at home. Otto sacked her. The BIC insisted she should be rehired. When Otto refused to do so a black ban was imposed on his business. The ban lasted for eight months. Interestingly, the unions said they would remove the ban if Otto hired the sacked girl's sister! Otto finally accepted the proposal.[5]

The final area of town life that the BIC concerned itself with was gambling and the sale of liquor. This was the province of the Police Department of New South Wales, but the BIC found a way to involve itself. Journalist Bob Bottom wrote an article for the influential magazine *The Bulletin* in 1963, saying, 'Because of union power, Broken Hill is almost free of the State's gambling and liquor laws.'[6] The article led to an inquiry into the New South Wales Police Force. Bob Bottom went on to become one of Australia's best known crime investigators.

IF NOT US, THEN WHO?

The BIC had strong views on how the town should operate that led it to take such an active role. The State and Commonwealth governments didn't have the statutory powers or institutions at this time to step in and address pricing and competition issues. The BIC adopted an *if-not-us-then-who* attitude to deal with issues in the town in the absence of regulatory bodies. It was a time when there was no umpire.

Over the next two decades Federal and State government organisations were created, in effect to play the umpire role the BIC had taken on. They include the Prices Justification Tribunal, the Fair Work Commission, the Australian Competition and Consumer Commission, the Equal Employment Commission, and authority being given to the High Court to enforce free trade between States.

For a small organisation, the BIC's reach was extraordinary. It willingly stepped into regulatory vacuums with its proclamations and bans, and this work was carried out with only elected delegates of the BIC. In many ways it was a model of efficiency in regulatory powers!

SOCIAL ENGINEERING ABANDONED

As Broken Hill High School students in the early 1960s, we would walk past the imposing Trades Hall building in Blende Street, where the BIC met. Today this fine building is heritage listed. We called it 'The Kremlin' but had little idea what happened in there, apart from boxing matches held in a big open space called The Stadium. Shorty O'Neil's biographer, W.A. Howard says, '… indeed it is difficult to think of a personal, social or municipal matter which was not considered in these offices'.[7]

Eventually, the BIC came to see that its social engineering had gone too far. When Shorty O'Neil retired in 1969, the winds of change began to blow. The BIC returned to its industrial roots, abandoning social engineering under the new BIC President, Joe Keenan. A hand-lettered sign on the door of the BIC offices '... informed all the world that the BIC would concern itself with industrial matters only'.[8]

The Barrier Industrial Council took on the umpire role in Broken Hill in matters relating to consumer prices, pub opening hours, employer rights to hire and fire, who could work where and when, compulsory unionism, company advertising and liquor and gambling hours. This social engineering role it took on didn't exist in other Australian towns and cities. It differentiated Broken Hill as a town like no other. The excursion into social engineering came to an end at the conclusion of Broken Hill's heyday.

Chapter 11

Multicultural Before We Knew the Word

From the 1930s Broken Hill saw multicultural shoots take hold, particularly in South Broken Hill. These multicultural families, steeped in their own culture, began to assimilate and contribute to the wider community. Relationships and friendships flourished between miners, neighbours, schoolchildren and the town's sporting and social clubs.

EARLY IMMIGRATION

The first settlers to Broken Hill were largely Australian born.[1] Many came from South Australia after the Kapunda copper mine closed in 1879. Of the men who came to Broken Hill many were originally from Cornwall, and many were members of the Methodist church. This explains why by 1908 there were seven Methodist churches in Broken Hill and Methodists represented over 30 per cent of the population.

Immigrants were attracted by the prospects of wealth from the rich line of lode in Broken Hill's mines. There's an expression in mining circles going back to the gold rush days that the most successful miners were those that provided the picks and shovels to dig for gold rather than those who panned for gold. In that same vein German immigrants like Emil Resch arrived from Germany and set up a brewery in Silverton and a cordial factory in Broken Hill. His brother set up Resch's Brewing in Sydney, which became Tooth's. As well, 38 Jewish families immigrated to Broken Hill and established shops like tailors, butchers, grocers and jewellery stores.[2] Dryens, the well-known drapery store opposite the courthouse, was established in 1894 by Jewish businessman Samuel Dryen.

In 1914 Australia went to war against Germany and Turkey, and on the first of January 1915 Broken Hill played an unusual role in the Turkish history part of the war. Two thought-to-be Turks attacked a train of 1200 picnickers travelling to Penrose Park outside of Broken Hill. It was the first attack on Australian soil in the war. Four picnickers were killed, and immediately afterwards police and volunteer riflemen arrived and killed the attackers. The two men were in fact of Afghan descent, not Turks at all. They lived in the Camel Camp in North Broken Hill. Thinking the men were Turks, an angry mob of residents descended on the Camel Camp that evening.

The camp Mullah managed to turn them away. The bodies of the two Afghani men who attacked the picnic train were taken to the town's mosque, but given their violent attack on the innocent picnickers, the cameleers disowned them and buried them in an unmarked grave. That same evening a mob also burned the German Club to the ground. They believed that Germany sympathisers had provided the weapons to the Turks. Today a memorial plaque acknowledges the picnic train attack at White Rocks not far from where the attackers themselves were killed.

Political upheavals in Yugoslavia, after the collapse of the Austro-Hungarian empire at the end of World War I, attracted Yugoslav men to Broken Hill. Many of the men had the idea that they would make money and then return home. Some brought their wives and children to Broken Hill. Others stayed and married local women.[3]

Immigration to Broken Hill was greatly reduced as employment on the mines fell in the Great Depression and World War II. Union policies to favour hiring local men came in at this time. When the mines began to prosper again, the union ban was lifted and the mines again hired multicultural miners.

The Santich and Ferry Families

It was in Piper Street, South Broken Hill, that Mata and Antica Santich opened their general store. Their customers were principally Yugoslav immigrants. The Santichs had come to Broken Hill from Prvic-Luka in

Croatia in the mid 1920s. One of their sons, Mero Santich, went on to run the workshops of the North Mine. My father grew up nearby and he and Mero were best friends as boys. Mero was captain of the junior soccer team of the Napredak Club. He married Phylis Ferry whose family came from Syria, now Lebanon, sometime in the 1880s or 1890s. The Ferry family had a prominent role in Broken Hill as both unionists and shop owners. Phylis's sister Rose had a supermarket in McCulloch Street and her brother Les owned the popular Orange Spot in Argent Street. Mero's son John and I became best friends in High School and have remained lifelong friends.[4]

POSTWAR TO 1970

Despite a significant community presence, the number of immigrants in Broken Hill was small in relation to the population. In the 1954 census there were 402 Italian born residents, 245 Maltese, 209 Yugoslavs and 126 Greeks, representing only 3 per cent of Broken Hill's population of 31,000. However, the census figure in 1954 excluded children who were born in Broken Hill to immigrant parents. When wives and children are included, that means that 10–15 per cent of the Broken Hill population was multicultural. Looked at this way, the multicultural share of the population starts to come into line with the community impact migrants were having.

The All Nations Hotel in Eyre Street opened in 1891 and was a popular pub for multicultural men. It was located close to the Yugoslav community's homes. The pub's name reflected the multicultural neighbourhood that was South Broken Hill from the earliest times in Broken Hill. The All Nations Hotel was featured in the films *Priscilla, Queen of the Desert* and *Last Cab to Darwin*.[5] It is now closed.

The ethnic communities began to establish their own clubs in Broken Hill. The Yugoslavs frequented the Napredak Club. There were also Italian, Greek and Maltese clubs. The Maltese residents established the Maltese Community Association of Broken Hill, a large enough community to warrant a visit by the Maltese Commissioner General in Australia in 1954. The Italian community increased in size in Broken Hill in the 1950s and a club building was opened in Crystal Street in 1960.

SOUTH BROKEN HILL: A YUGOSLAV HAVEN

South Broken Hill was divided from the other suburbs by the line of lode and a massive tailings dump known as Mount Hebbard. The population were called 'Southies'. There was a tribalism to the suburb that still exists today. In South Broken Hill there was a Yugoslav enclave in Piper Street and Hebbard Street, also home to the Napredak Club.

THE NAPREDAK CLUB

Napredak was the name given to the community organisation set up by Yugoslavs in 1936. The club featured the bowls game of bocce, a favourite game in their home country. The Napredak Club also had its own basketball and soccer teams.

In the 1950s the person most associated with the Napredak Club was Rudi Alagich OAM, also known as 'the sporting tailor' of Patton Street, South Broken Hill. We would go to Rudi's when we needed clothes for a special occasion. Rudi came from Dalmatia in Yugoslavia to Broken Hill in 1932. He became Chairman of the Napredak Youth Soccer Club and brought soccer to Broken Hill, gaining the nickname 'Mr Soccer'. He retired as an office bearer of the Napredak Club at age 90.

Rudi was an uncle to Robyn Ravlich, an ABC Radio journalist. In her autobiography Robin writes of the Napredak Club: 'The club played a pivotal role in our lives. For my mother, it provided the means to meet other women in her early years in Broken Hill.'[6] The club had a hall, a stage and bocce pitches. Robyn describes the club as 'a house of all nations', expanding beyond the Yugoslav community to the broader Broken Hill community by growing a wider membership.

The Kolinac Family

The Croatian Kolinac family were well known in Broken Hill as they had a paint shop in Argent Street and ran three pubs. Mary and Ivan Kolinac met in

Broken Hill. They had both been born in the town of Blato on the island of Korcula in Croatia. Mary came to Broken Hill at the age of nine with her family. Ivan came to Australia at the age of 19. The family home was in Piper Street, three houses away from the Napredak Club.[7]

During World War II Ivan was declared an alien because Croatia sided with Germany. He was taken to a custodial facility near Gosford for the duration of the war. Among the tasks he was given was to paint the Gosford hospital. This experience gave him the idea to set up a paint business in Broken Hill when he returned home after the war.

Mary went on to become a publican and the licensee of The Silver Spade (formerly The Criterion). Ivan and Mary became pillars of the Broken Hill community, Mary with her contributions to the CWA and the YWCA and Ivan with his membership and support of Rotary in Broken Hill and the South Broken Hill Football Club.

SOUTH BROKEN HILL FOOTBALL CLUB

There was nothing unusual about South Broken Hill winning the Australian Rules Football Premiership in 1958. Many called it the team of the century. What was unusual was the team's nationality composition compared to the other teams in the town. In the 1958 South's premiership team photo nine players of 19 came from European families, almost half the team. Five had Yugoslav names, Srzich, Mushan, Serich, Andrich and Pirak – one quarter of the team. They were outstanding players, with Serich and Pirak invited to try out and play in the Victorian Football League (VFL).

The 1967 South's premiership team included Mick Andrich and Oberon Pirak from the 1958 side, together with Ron Vlatko, Mick Bartulovich and John Dini, whose family was Italian. Players from immigrant families made up 20 per cent of the team. Pirak was much loved by his team members for his personal leadership and innovative captaincy.

A MODEL OF MULTICULTURALISM

It took less than a generation for immigrants from Yugoslavia living in South Broken Hill to assimilate. Their focus was on work, family, sport and community. Along with the other migrants who were drawn to Broken Hill, their cultural contributions greatly enriched the citizens of Broken Hill. In this period the town was truly a harbinger of things to come in cultural diversity.

In Broken Hill we had a strong model of multiculturalism supported by government programs to teach migrant adults to speak English. As well, leaders emerged from these ethnic community organisations who were respected across the city.

There was a tolerance and acceptance of difference at this time. The community felt proud of its multicultural leaders like Rudi Alagich and the Santich, Ferry and Kolinac families.

In the early 1970s the term multicultural became a popular description of how we were changing as a nation, welcoming migrant families to a growing economy. The Whitlam government Federal Minister for Immigration, the colourful Al Grassby, is often called 'the father of multiculturalism'. Broken Hill was ahead of the game – multicultural before the country knew the word.

Chapter 12

A Town Rich in Social Capital

> In the fifties the P&C Associations were an integral part of the school system ... hardly a weekend went by without some form of working bee arranged. There was never any shortage of parents for these working bees. Building or shifting tennis courts to more suitable sites, painting school benches, planting trees. You name it and the volunteers carried it out. The value of this voluntary work could not be estimated over the years.
>
> *Frank McLean, personal memoirs*

Communities that have high numbers of social clubs and voluntary associations, which provide opportunities for their citizens to help and support one another, and to socialise and build relationships and friendships, are communities that are said to be rich in social capital. This term was first advanced as a sociological concept in 2000 by Harvard sociologist Robert Putnam, representing the bonds of trust and reciprocity in a community. His research led him to conclude that many indicators of wellness in a community, like health and happiness, are closely linked to levels of social capital.[1]

Social capital is something to treasure. It was a major part of what made Broken Hill distinctive in the fifties and sixties. The breadth and depth of voluntary associations was remarkable. Residents were intensely engaged in the community, in some respects born out of isolation, but mostly because many in the community believed that volunteering was a good thing to do.

Broken Hill was a town of joiners and doers from its beginnings. In 1894 the Barrier Ranges Horticultural Society was formed, along with the Broken Hill Caledonian Society.

Two years later the Freemasons was started along with the Barrier Boys Brigade and the Broken Hill City Band in 1900. The Broken Hill Benevolent Society, a charity, opened its doors in 1901 and the Barrier Social Democratic Club formed in 1903. These community organisations were just a few of those that existed at the turn of the century. Broken Hill learned early and quickly not to expect too much from government – State, Federal or local.

Putnam found that communities varied greatly in their quantity of social capital. He noticed that there was a high watermark in the United States around 1960. His book *Bowling Alone: The Collapse and Revival of American Community* powerfully conveyed an image of low social capital in a community. That image captured widespread attention, the notion that someone would literally 'bowl alone', isolated with few connections to the community.

The level of social capital in a community is determined by factors such as the amount of discretionary time beyond the demands of work and family. Another factor is the extent of government service delivery. The more government provides welfare and other community services, the more likely there will be a crowding out of voluntary groups. Putnam attributes much of the decline in social capital in the United States around 1960 to television ownership, with more and more people using their leisure time to watch television in the evenings and on weekends. Social capital turns out to be heavily influenced by what else you can do with your time.

FAVOURABLE CONDITIONS TO THRIVE POSTWAR

Broken Hill was especially ripe for building social capital post-World War II. Its geography meant the town remained isolated from capital cities and the social and cultural activities they could offer. Miners were paid well and didn't need to work in second jobs. A high level of car ownership gave its citizens mobility around the town and its surrounding areas. The conditions for voluntary associations to thrive were extremely favourable. It's not surprising that the breadth and depth of voluntary associations were so great. The rich pool of social capital in Broken Hill from 1950 to 1970 was unmatched elsewhere in Australia and comparable to exemplars in the United States.

Spare time was available for clubs and societies. Miners were working the lowest hours of any group in Australia – a 35-hour week, with five shifts of seven hours. The end of day shift siren sounded at 3 pm. Their weekends were free for hobbies and recreation. Broken Hill had full employment in 1950. Miners' wages were high and, boosted by the lead bonus reaching record levels, comfortably supported a family. Not allowed to take jobs once they married, most married women had time to join voluntary associations once their children became more independent.

Robert Putnam marks the arrival of television in communities as a big factor impacting the social capital endowment of the community. Although television dates back to the 1940s in the United States, it wasn't until 1965 that Broken Hill got television. Good wages meant the take-up was high, and eventually television also began to compete with time for clubs and volunteering in Broken Hill.

THE DEPTH AND BREADTH OF BROKEN HILL BANDS

Today's visitors to Broken Hill are often surprised to see a sculpture in Sturt Park, two blocks from Argent Street, that is a tribute to the bandsmen of the *Titanic* who played heroically as the ship sank into the icy waters of the Atlantic. Bands had always been popular with musicians in Broken Hill. The bandsmen of Broken Hill raised the funds to commission the *Titanic* sculpture. It was unveiled in 1913. By the 1950s there were even more bands. When the Queen and Duke of Edinburgh visited Broken Hill in 1954, they were farewelled at the airport by the Cameron Pipe Band, the band playing 'Will Ye No Come Back Again'. The *Barrier Daily Truth* reported that the strains of the Cameron Pipe Band were said to 'express the sentiments of Broken Hill citizens'.[2] (The Queen didn't return to Broken Hill as my mother and her friends deeply hoped she would!)

The Barrier Industrial Council also had its own brass band and won the Australian Brass Band Championships on several occasions. The Salvation Army also had a band and, another, the Barrier Citizens Band, was formed in 1952. The bands of Broken Hill played on Anzac Day in the traditional march of servicemen and women along Argent Street.

CLUB LIFE

Clubs and pubs were the lifeblood of Broken Hill residents, but clubs rather than pubs had the added attraction of poker machines. In 1957 there were 12 registered clubs with 6300 members, which was 20 per cent of the population. The best known were the RSL Club for returned servicemen and the Barrier Social Democratic Club (the 'Demo Club') – a labour stronghold that included a circulating library and a book depot. Women were active in the Demo Club as well. The Sturt Club attracted people in commerce. The Broken Hill Club was patronised by professionals and mine managers, and the Musicians Club, the 'Musos', attracted music lovers. The Masons were strong in Broken Hill with 700 members.

The Country Women's Association offered social activities and supported vulnerable women. In 1952 they opened a hostel for country members and in 1959 the Mayor opened a new dedicated building in Crystal Street.[3]

Music and theatre were well supported in Broken Hill, including a choral group, the Silver City Singers, the Philharmonic Club and the Repertory Club. All had strong following. In November 1950 the Repertory Club staged their first costume productions, including the performance of the French seventeenth-century comedy *The Misanthrope*. As well, Broken Hill High School performed Gilbert and Sullivan productions in the town hall such as *The Pirates of Penzance* and *The Mikado*.

The Barrier Field Naturalists Club was widely celebrated for its role in creating the regeneration area to put an end to sand drifts. The club remained active in the fifties and sixties and took important initiatives such as protecting the rock art and natural environment of Mutawintji in the 1960s.

Gun clubs (seven at one point) and numerous sporting clubs rounded out the opportunities for social interaction. As well as football clubs and cricket groups, bowling clubs and tennis clubs were popular, as were horse and dog racing. The annual St Patrick's race day was an especially big social event for the town.

Golf also took off. The original golf club was built in 1921 by an army of town volunteers. The fairways were red dirt and the so-called 'greens' were made of oiled sand and crushed slag from the town's mining operations. It would be 60 years before the fairways of the Broken Hill Golf Club were converted to couch grass. Golfers share the fairways with the outback wildlife – kangaroos, emus and feral goats as well as the occasional turtle.

Ten pin bowling came to Broken Hill in 1961 when I was a teenager. It was incredibly popular for a time with rowdy team competitions. However, ten pin bowling faced a big challenge with the introduction of television in 1965. The bowling alley didn't survive.

WANING RECIPROCITY

Dad was the Secretary of the Alma Public School Parents and Citizens' Association for some four years. He described his experience with the P&C Association as it began to wane:

> ... after the fifties, a change took place in the education system. The P&C Associations, whilst still active, did not have the same influence that they had in years gone by. The Education Department whilst still needing the money raised did not require any input from the parents ... voluntary parent labour had finished by then.[4]
>
> *Frank McLean, personal memoirs*

Dad especially liked the parents being able to help fund items when the school budget wasn't available. But he didn't much like the headmaster's view that it was his money to spend as he pleased, when it was the P&C that had raised the money. This story illustrates how voluntary associations thrive under the right circumstances, and wane when reciprocity is removed. With the changes made by school principals on how P&Cs could contribute, volunteers like my father no longer felt that their contributions were valued and appreciated. The schools lost an engaged group of volunteers working to better the school.

My mother was a volunteer with Meals on Wheels when it began in Broken Hill in 1959, sponsored by the Rotary Club. Meals on Wheels would provide a prepared meal to the aged and infirm as a free service and delivered by their volunteers. In 1960 a home nursing service was added as well, under the auspices of Meals on Wheels. Mum was also a Red Cross volunteer. These organisations were important contributors to the social capital of Broken Hill. In 2025 Meals on Wheels was temporarily suspended due to waning numbers of volunteers.

ON A PAR WITH THE BEST

One simple way to measure social capital is by the number of voluntary associations active in a town. Some like Apex, Lions and Rotary you would expect to see in most larger towns, as well as the Salvation Army and active P&C Associations. Speculating, though, I doubt that you would see the same proportion of people working in volunteer organisations in comparable regional centres at the time. Broken Hill's isolation, full employment, a short working week with no need to take second jobs, meant that its citizens had time to get involved in organisations that interested them. Nor was government stepping into this community space. Broken Hill's citizens were filling that gap.

Robert Putnam's US exemplar of social capital in 1960 was a suburb of Chicago called Park Forest, with a population of 30,000 people. It was comparable in size to Broken Hill. Park Forest was termed a 'hotbed of participation'.[5] It had 66 community organisations. My rough count of Broken Hill's community organisations in 1960 was 52.[6] This suggests Broken Hill was on a par with the best social capital exemplar in the United States. I'm not surprised.

IT WASN'T ALL 'BEER AND SKITTLES'

My picture of a town rich in social capital isn't meant to imply that there wasn't a need for a safety net. Social disadvantage existed as did hardship and isolated people, including the elderly, and Indigenous people who lived on the fringes. I knew of mothers who struggled with social isolation. When a mother had young children, she typically wasn't working and often couldn't see a way of having community support and engagement until the children enrolled in kindergarten at age four. There were also the women who faced domestic violence and were reaching out to Lifeline for help from the time it opened in 1964 in Broken Hill, the fourth location in Australia.

The Yorkshire Television program in 1970 about Broken Hill – *Walled City* – included a segment shot at the Ladies Lounge of a pub. A dozen or more tables of older women were playing a game called 'Charity Bingo'. Some may have seen this as disparaging – that these women couldn't work and had nothing else to spend their time on. But it was in fact a positive message: these women were socially connected and raising money for charity. They were often the same women baking cakes for the CWA and helping out with the Red Cross, like my mother.

Many of the town's community, social and volunteer organisations are still in existence today. Alma Public School has an active P&C, South Broken Hill Football Club is still there and the Historical Society continues its work. The Barrier Field Naturalists have evolved as Landcare. Lifeline continues its support and the CWA was re-established in 2018 after a 25-year hiatus. But the town today is heavily supported by social welfare organisations. Broken Hill's population today is a much larger older demographic and there is a high level of economic disadvantage.

Broken Hill led Australia and its international peers in building strong, engaged communities through the 1950s and sixties. It was an early model of social capital building.

Chapter 13

Art Capital of the Outback

> May Harding is the thread between artists in Broken Hill. All roads of enquiry about Broken Hill's reputation in art lead to May Harding.[1]
>
> *Hester Lyon*

By the 1950s and 1960s Broken Hill was beginning to see itself as the art capital of the 'near' outback, a term to suggest it was accessible to the capital cities of Sydney, Melbourne and Adelaide. Art classes were being taught at the Broken Hill Technical College throughout this period and in 1961, 16 artists joined together to form the new Willyama Art Society. Local artists were developing distinctive styles to capture how they saw and artistically interpreted the landscape. Broken Hill was also home to New South Wales' oldest regional art gallery with paintings by English, Australian and local artists. In 2004 Broken Hill City Art Gallery moved to its new site on Argent Street, which had long been Sully's Emporium. When the gallery opened, the work of Indigenous artist Badger Bates was exhibited in the Frank McLean gallery. This gallery space was named after my father who loved the work of Broken Hill's artists.

MAY HARDING: PAINTER, NATURALIST AND BOTANIST

How the town laid the foundations for its artists to thrive is credited in part to Florence May Harding, a painter, naturalist and botanist, as well as a talented art teacher. May Harding was born in Silverton in 1908 before the family moved to Broken Hill. As a young woman she trained at the National Art School in Sydney. From an early age she collected native plants and became a member of the Barrier Field Naturalists Club, following botanist Albert Morris to become the club's secretary. She was a member of the Field Naturalists Club for 45 years. Her time in the field gave her a great appreciation of the beauty of the native flora of the West Darling region. She exhibited her paintings of wildflowers as early as 1922.

For 30 years she was the only art and botany teacher at the Technical College in Broken Hill. She taught children art at Saturday morning art classes and in her home.[2] Among the adult painters Harding taught and fostered was Sam Byrne, who only took up painting in his sixties after he retired. His paintings speak to earlier times when miners worked in difficult and dangerous conditions underground. A miner himself, he had been unable to work for a year after receiving an arm injury in a machine accident.[3] The line of lode overlooking Broken Hill is present in many of his paintings – painstakingly detailed panoramas of the township that led art critics to call him one of Australia's most genuine naïve painters. At the age of 80 Byrne had his first one-man show at the Rudy Komon Gallery in Paddington.

A collection of May Harding's work is included in the Broken Hill City Art Gallery. Her painting *Broken Hill Nocturne* is the cover image on this book. The line of lode overshadows the town as the sun is coming up. It's the one painting I associate most with Broken Hill for the way that it links the imposing mine-scape with the township. The painting conveys a strong sense of power and community. It was purchased by the Zinc Corporation in 1967 and then gifted to the gallery where it remains an important part of their collection.

Another painting of May Harding's that is in the gallery's collection is *Broken Hill Wild Flowers*. The wildflowers are a pop of colour in the desert landscape, colours not typically associated with the muted greens and brown of the arid zone. Along with the vibrant red Sturt Desert Peas are Grevillea blossom and yellow native daisies. Harding's flora paintings have similarities to the magnificent still life paintings done by Margaret Preston. *AnArt4Life* profile of May Harding in 2020 features these two paintings.[4] Its profile writer, Anne Newman, points out that Pro Hart used the colour palette of May Harding seen in *Broken Hill Wild Flowers*. That shouldn't come as a surprise given that he was a student of Harding's, along with others who went on to become prominent artists.

Although she exhibited for many years, May Harding did not attract critical acclaim in her own right. There is great diversity in May Harding's style and colour palette although her output of significant works is modest. Living and teaching in such an isolated place as Broken Hill left her out of the mainstream of the Sydney art scene where Margaret Olley, Grace Cossington Smith and Grace Crowley were gaining recognition.

May Harding was, however, recognised for her service to the community with a street in Broken Hill named after her. Her contributions in art, her study of native plants and service to sick and needy people in the community are set out in Jenny Camilleri's book *Some Outstanding Women of Broken Hill.*[5]

BRUSHMEN OF THE BUSH

By the mid-1960s there was growing excitement in Broken Hill about the way local artists were painting landscape. Sam Bryne's paintings were exhibited in a gallery opposite the Post Office and Pro Hart's work became very well known when he began to exhibit at the Barry Stern Gallery in Sydney.

My brother Ian and I visited Pro Hart at his home on several occasions. He had a significant collection of Australia's best-known artists. Artists were in the habit of swapping paintings with each other. Pro was generous with his time and would share stories of his various innovations, such as a trigger mechanism for a gun that the US army was testing. My first art purchase was a painting by Pro Hart called *After the Battle*, based on Banjo Patterson's poem of 'The Geebung Polo Club'. As a family we often talked about the art of Broken Hill, seeing the beauty of our arid landscape represented in ways we hadn't seen expressed before.

Pro Hart became the first Australian artist to receive a State funeral after he died in 2004. His family requested that it be held in Broken Hill. Pro Hart is widely considered to be the 'father of outback art'.

At the same time, the 'Brushmen of the Bush' emerged as a significant group of artists when the Willyama Art Society was founded in 1961. May Harding was a founding member of this formative group and served as Secretary. Among the 16 members of the society was the artist Joyce Condon, who won numerous art prizes including the coveted Rose Pollard Art Scholarship which allowed her to study the European masters in France, Italy and England. Her output was prolific and she would camp for weeks at a time in the outback with her paints and canvasses. She also taught art and in 1972 opened the first commercial art gallery in Broken Hill. Artists Hugh Schultz, Pro Hart, Eric Minchin, Tom Offord and Jack Absalom were also among the original 16 members of the Willyama Art Society.

I would see Jack Absalom from time to time as he rented a flat at the back of my uncle Arthur Reid's butcher shop in Argent Street before he became an artist. Then he was known as a kangaroo shooter and footy player for Centrals. Along with Jack, four other Brushmen of the Bush artists decided to exhibit together to highlight the diversity in interpreting the Broken Hill landscape. They included the radio broadcaster John Pickup, miner, artist and inventor Pro Hart, Hugh Schultz, also a miner, and Eric Minchin.

The Brushmen of the Bush label was the invention of a journalist for the *Women's Weekly* in 1973 writing about an exhibition by the Broken Hill artists. It was a remarkable piece of branding to make instantly recognisable a sizeable body of work by five artists. The name continues to resonate today in capturing their distinctive style.

ORIGIN STORY: THE LEGACY OF GEORGE AND MARY MCCULLOCH

The origin story of the regional art gallery in Broken Hill begins much earlier than the role that May Harding played from the 1930s. It began when in 1885 George McCulloch, a leader of the Syndicate of Seven, formed BHP. He became extremely wealthy from his one-seventh share in the syndicate. McCulloch retired to England in 1892 and married Mary Agnes Mayger in 1893.[6] He built up a major art collection with the wealth he acquired from the value of his BHP shares.

In 1904 the McCullochs donated three significant English paintings to a gallery that was to be created in the museum room at the Technical College. The unpacking of the paintings in front of the Mayor, Alderman Ivey, took place in July. The council had agreed to fund the cost of 15 pounds ($2200 in 2025) to make alterations to the new museum.[7] With the McCullochs' bequest of three major works, it was clearly a very good deal for the council to establish the first regional art gallery in New South Wales.

The three English paintings were *Lynmouth, North Devon* by James Webb (1867), *After the Bath* (1890) by Harriette Sutcliff, and *Memories* by John William Godward (1891). They remain in the gallery collection today.

After George McCulloch died in 1907 the considerable collection of 346 pieces that he and Mary had accumulated, excluding sculptures, was auctioned at the Royal Academy in London in 1909. One of the items, Lot 159, was Arthur Hacker's *Vae victis! The sack of Morocco by the Almohades, woe to the vanquished*, painted in 1890. Broken Hill City Council Alderman Dr James Booth heard that the McCulloch collection was being dispersed and contacted Mary Coutts-Mitchie, formerly Mrs George McCulloch. She ended up donating two paintings to the Broken Hill gallery, one by her new husband James Coutts-Mitchie called *Returning of the Hills*, and the other Hacker's *Vae victis!*

Vae victis! has been described as the most valuable painting in a regional art gallery in New South Wales. It is an arresting, grand painting that has been a feature of Broken Hill's art gallery for over a century.[8] It hangs upstairs in the permanent collection of the gallery.

Although philanthropy played a minor role in Australian life in the early 1900s, the story of the McCullochs is also interesting because it involved a philanthropic ask. The Broken Hill City Council asked for donations of paintings for the gallery. George's English wife Mary responded positively even though she had remarried.

THE MINING COMPANIES AND DIRECTORS

When we visited the Broken Hill Regional Art Gallery as schoolchildren, we were able to see a collection of fine Australian and international art. Many of the acquisitions were made by the mining companies of Broken Hill and in some cases by individual directors. Numerous paintings by esteemed Australian artists were also donated by the mining companies to the gallery. Frederick McCubbin's *Landscape*, Arthur Streeton's *St Marks Dome, Venice* and Margaret Preston's *Blue and Pink* are in the gallery's collection, all donated by the Zinc Corporation in 1948. In 1949 Zinc Corporation Director W.S. Robinson donated Rupert Bunny's *Portrait of a Young Woman*. North Broken Hill, together with Zinc Corporation, donated Hans Heysen's *Landscape with Cattle, 1942* in 1971. North also donated two paintings of May Harding in 1971, *Broken Hill Wild Flowers* n.d. and *Portrait of the Artist Sam Byrne* n.d.

In more recent years companies have shied away from sponsoring, let alone making gifts of art. One person who knew the art world and Broken Hill mining was Sir Roderick

Carnegie. As CEO of CRA Ltd he proposed to his board in the late 1970s that the company commission Fred Williams to do a series of paintings of the Pilbara district of Western Australia. CRA was mining iron ore in the Pilbara. The gift of Fred Williams' 18 gouaches and 13 paintings by CRA to the National Gallery of Victoria became the most significant corporate gift to the gallery.

THE MOVE TO SULLY'S EMPORIUM

The new Broken Hill City Art Gallery had once been Sully's, as grand a hardware store as most could imagine. It consisted of two floors and had a polished wooden balustrade and wide steps leading up to the first floor. Moving the Art Gallery into Sully's in Argent Street was an inspired move by the Broken Hill City Council. It made the gallery even more accessible to tourists and visitors and gave a new lease of life to an elegant and much-loved building in the town.

It was a move consistent with the circumstances the oldest regional gallery in New South Wales was facing. The collection was growing and now exceeds 2000 individual works. Visitor numbers to Broken Hill are growing as well. The vision to feature local art required a new space.

Today you can see contemporary and emerging artists in the downstairs gallery before you walk up the elegant staircase and enter a grand gallery space with outstanding paintings given to the gallery by the McCullochs, miners and artists. It's a space befitting the art capital of the near outback.

INDIGENOUS ART

The Broken Hill City Art Gallery has works by Indigenous artists such as Emily Kame Kngwarreye, Clifford Possum Tjapaltjari, Gloria Petyarre and Broken Hill Barkindji Elder Badger Bates.

Badger is a prominent artist in the West Darling and now Sydney, bringing a unique linocut style and visual storytelling to his art. In talking about his black and white linocuts of Barkindji country he says that often the country isn't colourful: 'For me, Australia is a black and white country.' He won the prestigious Red Ochre Award for lifetime achievement in 2024.

Today the Broken Hill City Art Gallery is a regular exhibitor of Indigenous art. A new generation of Indigenous artists are following in Badger Bates' footsteps, both building on his linocuts and developing their own artistic styles of painting and art installations. The Broken Hill City Art Gallery in partnership with Maari Ma, the Aboriginal Health Corporation, now also award an annual Indigenous art prize.

The 1950s and 1960s cemented Broken Hill's special status in art in New South Wales and Australia. Artists became household names, especially the 'Brushmen of the Bush'. The label stuck and has been of enormous value to art and tourism for the past 50 years.

Success has many parents and this expression resonates when reflecting on Broken Hill's success as the art capital of the near outback. Having an art gallery and a fine collection of local, Australian and international art was crucial as it was exceptional. Having patrons to acquire art and then donate it to the gallery was also exceptional. Having an art teacher, May Harding, who taught for 30 years, herself an accomplished artist, was rare in a remote, rural town. Finally, having a City Council that championed a local art gallery went beyond the remit of most councils 120 years ago. The desire to have art showcased and to have a gallery befitting the collection would have been a conundrum of the City Council for many years but the acquisition of Sully's Emporium was a successful and inspired move. The town set itself up for the future with space to exhibit significant emerging artists.

Chapter 14

Education Leader

No other town in Australia could claim outstanding leadership in school and tertiary education like that of Broken Hill in the 1950s and 1960s. The School of the Air were pioneers, developing the first virtual classroom for primary school students in the world. In secondary education Broken Hill High School was one of the largest schools not just in the state but in the Southern Hemisphere. Broken Hill High produced outcomes not seen in public schools for decades to come. The town also supported tertiary education with its own university. With a population of only 30,000, this was matched only by the University of New England in Armidale but that served a much larger catchment area extending to the whole New England region and North Coast.

SCHOOL OF THE AIR: A CLASSROOM OF ONE

The vast distances between sheep stations and towns with schools in the West Darling made it impossible to offer primary education to station children. For almost a century, these primary school children living in remote towns and sheep stations were homeschooled, supported by a correspondence program set up by the NSW Department of Education. This all changed when School of the Air was established in 1956 in Broken Hill. It was also made available to isolated children beyond New South Wales in southern Queensland and South Australia. Mrs Phyllis Gibb, a classroom teacher, was appointed as the first principal. She also taught a Sunday School program on radio 2BH Broken Hill.[1] She later received a Member of the British Empire Award (MBE) for her service.

It was an ingenious initiative. School of the Air partnered with the Royal Flying Doctor Service (RFDS) to be able to utilise their high frequency (HF) radio (shortwave) on the RFDS doctor network in Broken Hill. The RFDS was another Australian innovation and was set up in 1936 in Broken Hill. The RFDS served the outback people of the West Darling, with a radio network to assess and diagnose patients' symptoms and then, if needed, fly a doctor to the scene of an accident or a critically ill patient. Without the RFDS's radio network, there could not have been a School of the Air.

Students would listen to Mrs Gibb open the school day and reply to her questions on their transceiver system on their property. School of the Air lessons supplemented the previous system of written correspondence lessons that had to be completed and then mailed to Sydney.

I often listened in to School of the Air on visits to Woolcunda Station, located between Broken Hill and Wentworth. Rob Seekamp of Woolcunda Station was himself a student of School of the Air at that time. His mother Hilary created a classroom space for Rob in their house and made sure the transceiver was operating. It was a classroom of one, an educator's dream – a 'school' of one in the station but virtually connected to a wide cohort of children on other remote stations in the West Darling. They couldn't see each other's faces but they could hear one another as they engaged with Mrs Gibb.

School of the Air tried to recreate an authentic school atmosphere by beginning each day with the school song. Pupils had six half-day lessons each week including recorder lessons for music. Students met each other face to face twice a year, once during Education week where they sang and performed and at a Christmas party for children and parents held at Penrose Park near Silverton.

Some 200 students a year were enrolled in School of the Air. It provided educational opportunity for children on remote sheep stations hundreds of kilometres from Broken Hill. School of the Air is fondly remembered by the thousands of students who had the first virtual classroom in the world, a pioneering initiative in providing educational opportunity for remote students.

School of the Air continues today in Broken Hill and in Hay in the Riverina region. The program delivery has been replaced with telephone and email instead of the shortwave radio network of the past.

A FIRST-CLASS PUBLIC EDUCATION

At the time I began as a student at Broken Hill High School in 1959, I had no idea that the high school was relatively so large.[2] Student numbers continued to grow and in 1974 a second high school, Willyama, was opened in Broken Hill, one that my sister Judith attended.

Being a large high school brought several advantages, in particular the number of diverse course offerings and electives. In our first year of high school, we were divided into a technical stream that finished at the Intermediate Certificate or a classical stream that went through to the Leaving Certificate. In the classical stream boys and girls were able to study Latin and French, mathematics one and two and physics and chemistry.

Broken Hill High's size may help explain why there were so many highly qualified teachers at the school in the 1960s, as well as the fact the NSW Education Department often placed newly qualified teachers in regional schools. Now, and for the past several decades, it's become harder and harder to attract teachers to remote places like Broken Hill.

HIGH QUALITY TEACHING

Our teachers, with only a few exceptions, were passionate about teaching their chosen subject. They encouraged us to pursue our interests and steered us towards our strengths. We were encouraged by our teachers to set aspirations.

Robin Ravlich, a Broken Hill High student in the 1960s, provides a wonderful example of staff/student engagement in her book *Skywriting*. She says that her French teacher, Harvey Clarkson, '… invited the senior class to his house for special evenings, where we listened to French discs (records), ate garlic snails imported in tins and read French magazines. In our final term, there may have even been a glass or two of claret.'[3]

I had a similar experience. One of my favourite teachers was Quentin Willis who taught history. He invited the history honours class to his house where we debated issues like the causes of World War II, although I don't recall any claret being offered! When he wanted to bring the evening to a close, he would play 'God Save the Queen' on his record player and we would quickly file out and go home. In today's world going to a teacher's home wouldn't be allowed, yet these experiences provided an extraordinary learning environment.

Quentin Willis encouraged us to develop logical arguments that could be defended, and to present our argument well. In class he would say, 'Let's hear your view, McLean. I want to hear it in a loud, clear, resonant and stentorian voice.' I would have had to look up the word stentorian at the time, and I've never forgotten its Oxford Dictionary definition: *Stentorian:*

adjective (of a person's voice) loud and powerful. Learning to speak well and speak up was sound advice, then and now, on how to communicate effectively.

Don Neville arrived at Broken Hill High School as a 21-year-old music teacher. From 1960 to 1963 he opened up the world of performance to the High School and the greater Broken Hill community with Gilbert and Sullivan productions. They were musical performances my classmates remember fondly and an introduction to the art of musical production.

Sandra Kanck, also a student in the 1960s, wanted to study Elective Music. Don tried to persuade Sandra and others to think very carefully about this choice because of its huge demands. Sandra went ahead and studied Elective Music and did well. She recently told me that she appreciated Don's candour in outlining the demands of the course of study.[4]

Don met Merran Nankivell, his wife to be, in Broken Hill and years later they moved to Ontario, Canada, where Don became a Professor of Music at Western Ontario University. Merran remarked recently that for all Don's academic interests and success 'Broken Hill High School and community have always remained his first love'.[5]

These were only a few of the teachers who brought passion and knowledge to their teaching at Broken Hill High School. Educators debate what is needed for a first-class education today. They keep coming back to having a demanding curriculum that develops literacy and numeracy, inspires, and doesn't dumb down the subject matter. Having teachers who are trained in their subject is vitally important. Today it is reported that up to 40 per cent of maths teachers haven't been trained to teach maths.

THE CLASS OF 1963

Our fifth-year class was 67 in number, 47 boys and 20 girls. That's a long way from gender parity and reflects a time when many girls were told by their parents to leave school at 15 and get a job. There was an assumption that they would marry young and stay home to raise children. Some of the brightest students I remember at Broken Hill High were girls who left school before matriculation. If they had pursued careers, it would have made the performance of our class look even more stellar.

In 1963 in New South Wales more students were starting to go to university with the aid of Commonwealth Scholarships. From the class members that the alumni organisers have been able to track down, over 50 per cent undertook tertiary education. It's a surprisingly high figure for that time, one that confirms Broken Hill High School was preparing students for professional careers.

Of 67 graduates of the high school from my fifth-year class, 14 went into teaching, three into nursing and one studied medicine; 11 studied mining, metallurgy or mechanical engineering; four did accounting and one studied architecture; three received doctorates in science-based disciplines; one received first-class honours in econometrics together with an

MBA, one gained first-class honours in geology/chemistry; and two went to the Royal Military College, Duntroon.

Classes just ahead and just behind mine seemed no less talented than ours. When you seek to explain why the classes in these years performed so well, clearly one of the most important factors was our teachers. They opened our horizons and encouraged us to undertake tertiary study, to prioritise getting a degree.

We also had what I think of as an 'X factor' – that hard to define variable – that a proud, well-resourced remote school was no bar to academic achievement.

TERTIARY STUDY

Broken Hill was fortunate to have its own Technical College where students could work in the day and study in the evening. It transitioned to full degree programs, including master's degrees in 1959, when the University of New South Wales opened the WS and LB Robinson College campus opposite the Zinc Lakes. CRA Chairman Maurie Mawby and CEO John Ralph studied at the 'tech', as did chemist and head of metallurgy at Zinc Corporation Bruce Rawling.

Among my classmates who studied at the WS and LB Robinson College was Trevor Watters who became head of metallurgy for North Broken Hill and later Pasminco. Craig Bermingham did a mining degree and went on to become General Manager of North Broken Hill and then Pasminco.

John Dennis did a BSc (mathematics/chemistry) and worked at Broken Hill South. Ian Wright and John Richards graduated with BSc degrees in mechanical engineering. Leslie Bills received a first-class honours degree in geology and chemistry, the first person studying in Broken Hill to receive first-class honours.

It was fitting for the school to be named the WS and LB Robinson College. The Robinsons played an important role in founding Zinc Corporation and New Broken Hill Consolidated. They wanted to see tertiary education pursued in the Broken Hill community. They saw this as a community investment commensurate with a fabulously rich orebody.

The WS and LB Robinson College closed in 1984 when the remaining major mining operations finished. The model depended on students being able to work at the mines and study. The college was a major asset to Broken Hill and one the city was sorry to lose although today there is a new way to study for a degree while living at home in Broken Hill. That is through the Country University Centre (CUC) Far West campus in Broken Hill. It is on the site of the old RSL building across from the railway station. It's an initiative by Duncan Taylor from Cooma that is fast catching on in other regional centres. Students have access to computers, tutorial rooms and conferencing facilities. There are now over one hundred students in Broken Hill studying for degrees through CUC.

The New South Wales Government often seemed to be missing in action when it came to meeting community needs in Broken Hill. However, that wasn't the case for primary and secondary education. School of the Air played a critical role in primary education on remote stations and the Education Department made it attractive for good teachers to come to live and teach in Broken Hill.

The town is singled out for its exceptionalism in so many areas, most often when it relates to mining and unions. But its role as a leader in education warrants inclusion in the list of factors that made the city a town like no other.

Chapter 15

Punching Above Its Weight

> Wallace Stegner, famous as the writer of the American West and the 1972 winner of the Pulitzer Prize, argued that talent can't be taught. But it can be awakened.[1]

Awakening talent is a powerful metaphor. It conveys the idea that talent is nurtured. Broken Hill provided a multitude of platforms to enable budding talent to develop and have impact beyond the town. Broken Hill, so isolated from major cities, has always been proud of its talent. Locals love saying, 'You know they got their start in Broken Hill' – especially if the talented person went on to a national or international stage. In its heyday period, the town of only 30,000 seemed to bulge with talent – from mining and entrepreneurial talent to artistic and broadcasting talent, to academic and research talent.

If you search for famous people raised in Broken Hill, you'll find names of actors like Chips Rafferty. I met Chips quite by accident when we were both on the Caribbean island of Jamaica. Chips was an actor in the movie *Skullduggery*, starring Burt Reynolds and Susan Clark. I was a star-struck extra, a cricket player filmed for a flash of a second, along with some Columbia University Rugby friends. Chips proudly declared his Broken Hill origins and was surprised to meet another Broken Hill boy far from home.

June Bronhill became famous as an opera singer in London, but she'd grown up in Broken Hill. Her name was June Gough but she chose the stage name of Bronhill, a shortened version of Broken Hill and her tribute to the town that had nurtured her. Nursing sister Vivian Bullwinkle, who grew up in Broken Hill and trained at the local hospital, was honoured in 2023 with a bronze statue at the Australian War Memorial. Irene Drummond, another nursing sister affiliated with Broken Hill, was honoured for her heroism in World War II. She was one of the 22 nurses who, during their Australian war service on the Indonesian island of Bangka, were murdered by the advancing Japanese army.

Well-known writers like Ion Idriess OBE and Dame Mary Gilmore also lived in the Broken Hill area, as did activist and advocate for women Nydia Edes. The earlier chapter 'Art Capital of the Outback' illustrates the wealth of talent of Broken Hill painters, and how the town nurtured their gift.

PATHWAY TO MINING LEADERSHIP

Broken Hill was home to an extraordinary amount of mining talent – people who went on to become the country's national and international mining leaders. In Australia, mining leaders are celebrated by their peers. The highest award is the Institute Medal of the Australasian Institute of Mining and Metallurgy (AIMM). From 1951 to 2010 the Institute Medal was won on 10 occasions by a mining leader who had worked in Broken Hill, making Broken Hill by far the single most important mining centre in Australia. Among the winners of the Institute Medal who lived and trained in Broken Hill, and then went on to greater things, were Sir James Foots, Sir Frank Espie and Sir Russell Madigan. Don Carruthers was recognised for contributions to exploration. Bruce Rawling was the winner of the AIMM President's Medal for his contributions to flotation technology. Many others also went on to have CEO roles at Australian mining companies, like Terry Palmer and his brother Tony, Vince Gauci and his brother George, and John Dini.

This distinguished list is only the tip of the iceberg of mining and metallurgy leaders who were raised or trained in Broken Hill between 1950 and 1970. I've selected four of their stories to illustrate how it was that the mining companies in Broken Hill helped to launch their illustrious careers.

John Ralph AC

John Ralph began working as a clerk at Zinc Corp/ NBHC in 1949 while he was studying accounting.

My father worked with him in the offices of the mine. He admired John for his work rate and his intense curiosity about people. John would take time to engage throughout the workday with mine managers and people from different parts of the mine and mill. Some staff would grumble, saying, 'Ralphie talks all day and doesn't get any work done.' My father would defend John, saying he would see John working back at night, when there was no one to disturb him. John ended up with a unique perspective on Zinc Corp's Broken Hill operations because of all the time he put into engaging with people at the mine.

His accountancy training in the mines of Broken Hill prepared him well for promotions into top jobs in general management. CRA's Chairman, Maurie Mawby, hired John on matriculation. Later John transferred to CRA in Melbourne. He went on to become CEO of CRA in 1987. He became involved with the biggest issue the company faced, that of how to finance the rich set of growth options the company had. John championed supporting employees, giving them greater responsibility, and making safety an ongoing and priority issue. He later chaired the Commonwealth Bank and Pacific Dunlop, was Deputy Chair of Telstra and a director of BHP.

Leigh Clifford AO, Roger Massy-Greene AM and Peter Coates AO

Leigh Clifford got his start in mining as a summer student at Zinc/NBHC and then later as a graduate engineer. He progressed from an assistant surveyor role to working in rock mechanics, underground maintenance and finally to a senior mining engineer position.

When I asked Leigh to describe his time working in Broken Hill, he talked about people and front-line leadership rather than mining techniques or machinery. The learning that Leigh gained from his time in Broken Hill was a pathway to leadership. He felt enormous respect for the capability of the miners and took away the importance of focusing on safety. He'd received training from experienced hands like Alister McLean, who was head of training and also my uncle. Leigh got to see how front-line supervision had to meet the demands for production output while always prioritising safety. These experiences were important preparation for the career challenges to come. Years later, working in the coal industry and negotiating with experienced union leaders, he realised he'd had as much time underground as many of them. That added to his credibility in tough negotiating situations. Later again, as CEO of Rio Tinto and Chair of Qantas, his management development in Broken Hill shone through.

Leigh also worked with Assistant Underground Mine Managers at Zinc/NBHC like Roger Massy-Greene AM. Roger was another mining engineer who had rotated through roles in rock mechanics, underground maintenance and ventilation, and by the age of 27 he had risen to the role of Assistant Underground Manager. In Roger's role, he was legally responsible for the lives of 300 miners. Giving such responsibility so early in a graduate's career was a hallmark of the talent development path in Broken Hill mining.

Peter Coates AO, another Institute Medal winner like Leigh Clifford, had a similar rapid progression in Broken Hill's heyday mining period. He'd also been promoted to Assistant Underground Manager very quickly. Each of these young men got what was called a 'mine manager's ticket'. This was a qualification requiring two years' experience working in a mine, including working at the face.

Like the illustrious career path of Leigh Clifford, Roger Massy-Greene and Peter Coates also went on to have distinguished careers, Roger as Chairman of Excel Coal and Peter as Glencore Australia's Managing Director and Chair of Santos Limited. These three were among the legion of executive trainees at Broken Hill, more than capable of taking on senior leadership roles in other Australian mining companies.

A WOMAN WHO BROKE THE MOULD: TESS ALFONSI AO

Broken Hill was considered a man's town in the mining industry, and not seen as a profession for women to enter. One woman broke that mould. Her name was Tess Alfonsi AO. She was bitten by the prospecting bug and bought and ran the Triple Chance Mine near Broken Hill from 1927 until the late 1970s. It was appropriately named as she mined mica, feldspar and beryl, giving her three chances to strike it lucky on world markets. When her stockpiled ore was stolen or claim jumpers tried to take her mining leases, Tess famously defended her property with a .303 rifle in hand.[2] She was later recognised by the Broken Hill TAFE as an outstanding female mining student and also awarded an AO in 1980 for her philanthropy to Broken Hill charities.

CAREER PATHWAYS TO THE PROFESSIONS

From the 1950s students increasingly finished secondary school in Broken Hill and began training in professions like law, medicine and engineering, as well as illustrious academic careers and journalism. Although there are many people who shone, I've chosen three to highlight.

Dimitri Caplygin

Although many in Broken Hill remember Dimitri Caplygin and his brother Serge as superb gymnasts, Serge told me that Dimitri was also an excellent pianist and that he started the model aircraft club at the Police Boys Club. Dimitri was the junior light heavy weightlifting champion of Australia.[3]

Today Dimitri is best recognised as a world-class inventor. He was the holder of six patents granted by the US Patent Office. The first, in 1978, was for a disc brake assembly unit used in the automotive industry. His employer Girlock was awarded a contract to supply a complete braking system to General Motor's Chevrolet Division. He turned his hand to a new field in the 1980s, that of the use of computer aided design (CAD) to design reefer machines for the shipping container industry.

In 2000 he filed a patent related to the enhancement of neurophysiological processes. His patent was focused on computer science to manage dyslexia. He set up a company called Cellfield International to commercialise the technology. The Cellfield reading program has 45 centres around the world to improve the reading skills of dyslexic students. Dimitri passed away in 2019.

Geoff Brennan

Geoff Brennan was Dux of his year at Broken Hill High in the early 1960s, as well as school captain and head of the debating team. Helen Palmer, who was in my year at school and on the debating team with Geoff, told me that he was always the first speaker, who led off powerfully and had a presence and maturity well beyond his years.[4]

Geoff studied economics at ANU and went on to academic appointments at the University of Virginia and the University of North Carolina. He wrote two books with Nobel Laureate James Buchanan, *The Power to Tax*[5] and *The Reason of Rules*.[6] James Buchanan lauds Geoff Brennan's contribution to writing *The Power to Tax*.[7] Brennan and Buchanan's work advanced what is called Public Choice theory in economics, an important field that brings economic analysis to political decision-making.

Geoff Brennan's research was widely cited, putting him in the top 1 per cent of economists worldwide. He passed away in 2022.

Robyn Ravlich

Robyn Ravlich had a 35-year career with the ABC as a radio broadcaster. She received national and international recognition for her innovations in radio broadcasting where she was described as a 'radio poet'. In her own description she said she was like an artist – 'someone who paints with sound'. Sounds from birds, music, whales and conversation were incorporated to 'construct worlds' for her listeners. Some related to political issues such as refugees from the *Tampa* in her program 'Raft of the Medusa'.[8]

Wondering what led a young woman from a multicultural family in Broken Hill into a career as a celebrated radio broadcaster, I found her explanation for this in the first chapters of her autobiography, *Skywriting*.[9] She describes how important radio was to our lives in a country town, a time before television arrived in 1965.

At the Broken Hill High School, she thrived with what she called her 'inspirational teachers'. Robyn's interests in writing, acting, debating and poetry were all encouraged at the high school, aided by having a portable tape recorder to practise French pronunciation and fluency, a gift from her parents that led to 'a nascent love of the recorded voice and sound'.

A Barrier Industrial Council Scholarship allowed Robyn to attend Sydney University and study arts. She became a poet before she joined the ABC. She attributes growing up in Broken Hill in the 1950s and 1960 as foundational to her career.

SPORTING HEROES GALORE

Who was the most significant sporting export from Broken Hill is likely to be highly contested. Broken Hill people are sporting 'tragics' and very loyal to their teams. During this period of the 1950s and 1960s there were sporting teams galore in Broken Hill to choose from. In athletics in this era John Cann won the Stawell Gift in 1949 and Stan Baldwin won the Bendigo Thousand Foot Race in 1951. In sports, as with other endeavours, Broken Hill wanted to see their best competing on bigger stages.

Ron Serich

For me, a football tragic as well, the most significant sportsperson in this period was Ron Serich who emerged from South Broken Hill Football Club to be the first footballer to play for the hallowed Victorian Football League. Ron had been named the Broken Hill league's best and fairest in 1959 and in 1960 was the leading goalkicker. He debuted with Richmond in the 1961 season, playing 28 games over three seasons.

I once met Ron at a South Football Club reunion in Adelaide. My memory of Ron had been that of a tall full forward who could take the big mark in the goal square with opposition players hanging off him, all trying to punch the ball away. To my surprise Ron

> was only a little taller than me. He had an amazing leap for his height of only 180 centimetres.

Ron Serich paved a way for other footballers to follow, including Stephen Hywood, George Lakes and Chris Lynch. All three went on to play in the VFL at this time.

Broken Hill punched above its weight as a talent exporter. In a mining town you would expect to see mining and metallurgy talent shine. But talent was also exported in many other fields, as well as sport. The ethos of the town was that its best could compete with the best from anywhere.

Chapter 16

Edge of Sundown

Over many decades of mining in Broken Hill, its townspeople have long contemplated what their future might look like when the mines run out. Historian Robert Solomon, in his 1988 book *The Richest Lode*, wrote about the efforts being made to enlist the support of the New South Wales Government when Broken Hill's mines closed. He concluded that, 'Self-help seems the best answer on the edge of sundown.'[1] It's a point of view that sits comfortably with the independent nature of the people of Broken Hill. They knew forging a new future for their isolated town was going to be up to them.

Solomon included a chapter in his book called 'After The Mines'.[2] He correctly predicted that tourism would be the town's future. The desert flora and fauna, the attractiveness of the grand classical buildings and wide streets named after minerals and ores, along with opportunities to learn about mining history and to visit Indigenous cultural places like Mutawintji were all golden tourist drawcards for the town. Solomon also supported the expansion of cropping and grazing on Lake Tandou in the Menindee Lakes, although that dream came to an end in 2018 when Tandou sold its water rights back to the Commonwealth under the water buyback scheme.

ERASING HISTORY

There are no guarantees of a mining town's future when its mines run out. The town of Radium Hill, 110 kilometres from Broken Hill and the site of a uranium mine, once had a population of 1000 but is now a ghost town. The town of Wittenoom in Western Australia, where asbestos was mined, is called an 'erased town'. And it is hard to imagine that Silverton, nearby to Broken Hill, once had a Resch's brewery at Umberumberka Creek and a population of 3000 people in the 1880s. The grand two-storey Bank of Australasia in Silverton was moved block by block to a new resting place in William Street in Broken Hill in 1904, another way of erasing history.

When a mine closes in a community a 'front door' shuts. When a new door opens it's most likely to be because there are assets that can be used in new ways or capabilities that can be harnessed to meet new markets. The community itself needs to get involved to secure its future. In Broken Hill's case there is plenty of evidence to suggest that the community is hard at work to create a future for the next generation.

MINING LIVES ON

Broken Hill has stayed the same in many respects while it also takes on some new directions. Mining hasn't gone away, and, as many expected, tourism has become an important contributor; the arts have also grown and are integral to the tourist offering. The city remains a centre for health care in the West Darling and there is a growing need for social services. New energy industries are emerging, and consistent with Broken Hill as a tourism and service centre, new businesses are opening.

It comes as a surprise to hear that mining provides almost a thousand jobs, over 12 per cent in 2023–24 of the town's jobs.[3] That puts mining on a par with the number of jobs tourism generates in the town. After Pasminco shut down mining operations in March 2002, the mine was sold to Perilya. Today Perilya is mining from its Southern Operations underground mine and the Potosi/Silver Peak mine.

The discovery of cobalt near Broken Hill led Cobalt Blue Holdings to plan a significant investment with 400 jobs. With the oversupply of cobalt at present that plan is now being scaled back. The cobalt price has extreme volatility making investment plans difficult. A distinguishing aspect of Cobalt Blue Holdings' operation is that unlike the major producer, the

Democratic Republic of Congo, it adheres to internationally recognised child labour laws to combat modern day slavery.

Cobalt is included in the Labor Government's strategic minerals reserve. It will be interesting to see whether the government underwrites mine development at Cobalt Blue. The region has other critical minerals like beryllium and antimony. One of the arguments for keeping the Port Pirie smelter open is that antimony is recovered in the minerals separation process.

There is an adage in mineral exploration that the best place to look for a new mine is near an old mine. A significant level of ongoing exploration that could identify a hidden orebody may ultimately lead to a new mine in Broken Hill.

THE ACCESSIBLE OUTBACK

Tourism is vitally important to Broken Hill's economy. In the two years to June 2024 the town averaged 729,000 visitor nights. If we take a three-night stay as an average, that's 243,000 unique visitors per year. Tourism accounts for 12 per cent of employment in Broken Hill and has been growing modestly at about 2 per cent per annum – not as high as the rest of New South Wales tourism growth of 3 per cent per annum.[4]

Broken Hill has a strong value proposition as a tourist destination. Visitors are seeking a link with an historic past, visiting the Miners Memorial above the line of lode, driving to the ghost town of Silverton or touring the Royal Flying Doctor base. Broken Hill's art galleries and shops selling mineral collections are popular. Others want to see where films like *Priscilla, Queen of the Desert* or *Mad Max* were made. Now there's a hugely successful concert, the three-day Mundi Mundi Bash, where concertgoers camp overnight. In 2024 14,000 people attended the Mundi Mundi Bash. Broken Hill is the 'accessible outback' as the tourism promotion suggests, as the city can be reached in a day from Sydney and Melbourne. Broken Hill is also the take-off point for adventure tours to remote destinations like the UNESCO World Heritage listed Lake Mungo and the Birdsville Track.

Professional groups like the Australian Mining History Association held their annual conference in Broken Hill in August/September 2025. Delegates attended the conference and made field trips to mine sites and Silverton. About half the papers featured Broken Hill mining as their subject. Leigh Clifford delivered the keynote address. It's hard to think of a better place to talk about mining history in Australia, other than Kalgoorlie with its Diggers and Dealers conference each year.

THE CHALLENGES OF HEALTH CARE AND SOCIAL SERVICES

Broken Hill has changed in an important respect in 75 years. It has gone from being economically advantaged, one of the places with the highest incomes in Australia in its heyday, to a socioeconomically disadvantaged community. This brings new challenges for the health and social services sector. It is far and away the biggest employer, providing over 20 per cent of jobs. Broken Hill is a health and hospital centre for all of the West Darling. The Royal Flying Doctor Service is based in Broken Hill, but the nearest major hospital in New South Wales is in Dubbo, almost 700 kilometres by air.

There are several other factors that explain why Broken Hill has high health and social service needs. First, it is an older population demographic, which always has more health needs. Broken Hill has 32 per cent more of its population aged over 60 years than the rest of Australia. With socioeconomic disadvantage comes a range of physical and mental health conditions. In 2023 The Benevolent Society expanded its presence in Broken Hill to meet the demand for allied health services such as occupational therapy, covered by the NDIS.[5]

A final factor is that the Indigenous population in Broken Hill has grown and has special health needs. Maari Ma is an Aboriginal health corporation that aims to improve health access for Aboriginal people. It has an excellent record in service delivery, winning the confidence not only of Indigenous people and NSW Health, but philanthropic funders like the Cages Foundation and the Paul Ramsay Foundation.

ENERGY FUTURES

Broken Hill has sunshine, wind and alienated land from overgrazing and disused mines. Over a billion dollars of capital has been earmarked for three projects, the Silverton Wind Farm, the Broken Hill Solar Farm and, also under consideration, the Hydrostor compressed air project. It would provide a back-up power supply to Broken Hill. The Silverton Wind Farm project will create 10 full-time jobs. The Hydrostor project will create 700 jobs in its construction phase, and 35 jobs when operational.[6] Carbon farming may eventually offer economic and climate benefits as well, but the jury is still out on its potential. If Broken Hill could attract more large-scale projects related to renewable energy like solar farms and wind farms, energy could become a driver of the local economy and future job growth. Broken Hill has some of the highest levels of solar radiation in New South Wales making it an ideal site for solar power generation. However, it is limited by grid capacity.

FOUNDATION BROKEN HILL AND CEF FAR WEST

Foundation Broken Hill was started to support new enterprises to grow and replace the lost mining jobs. The foundation was started by Broken Hill raised Vince Gauci, a former CEO and a local hero, who was concerned about the future of Broken Hill when mining ceased. Former Broken Hill people contributed to the start-up phase of the foundation some 20 years ago. It is an important community asset and another example of Broken Hill people taking initiatives to secure the town's future.

CEF Far West, the local committee that raises money for student grants under the umbrella of the Country Education Foundation of Australia, supports Broken Hill's students to go on to tertiary and post school study.

Both Foundation Broken Hill and CEF Far West are important community assets and another example of initiatives to provide pathways to future jobs for the town.

IMPERIAL LAKES NATURE PARK

The Imperial Lakes are just out of town on the Barrier Highway. They were part of North Broken Hill's mining operations. Landcare Broken Hill purchased the Imperial Lakes, a 59-hectare property. The community-based conservation area includes a regeneration reserve, a propagation nursery and a seed bank. Volunteers plant and maintain native vegetation and build walkways. Simon Molesworth AO KC and his wife Lindy, who grew up in Broken Hill, are leading the initiative. The Imperial Lakes Nature Park will be a showcase of arid zone regeneration, a tranquil place for visitors and an education centre for schoolchildren. The thick bush that explorer Captain Charles Sturt described in passing through the Barrier Ranges in 1844 will once again be on display.

BUILDING ON ITS STRENGTHS

Towns and cities that have lost their economic base face a challenge to grow again and thrive. Some communities had a view that it might be best to pack up and move on, and not bother with government-led job creation schemes to keep people in a town. Fortunately, some cities decided to find ways to build on their strengths after their major employer closed or moved elsewhere. The city of Pittsburgh in the United States is a great example. After steelmaking closed, it has emerged as a tech centre based largely on its two universities, Carnegie Mellon and the University of Pittsburgh.

Taking stock of assets is a powerful way to uncover ways to grow. Broken Hill is edging to an asset-based view of itself. Use of Crown land for a wind farm, repurposing a disused mine for energy storage and hosting music festivals on the vast Mundi Mundi Plains are all examples of taking stock of a community's assets. Each example creates new jobs.

A community is defined by its physical and social capital. Broken Hill has always had large endowments of both. These natural and human endowments are allowing the town to be reinvented. As Robert Solomon predicted, these opportunities depended on the self-reliance of the townspeople, making the best use of their assets and capabilities. As will always be the case for any community, new challenges will emerge.

For Broken Hill there are two that must be addressed. One is the demands of an ageing demographic that will test the town's supply of adequate care facilities. The second challenge is the disturbing lead levels being measured in Broken Hill children. Data driven health is allowing research and pathways to solutions, but there is still much to learn about the lead levels sustained in mining communities.[7]

Although Broken Hill's population has fallen from its heyday period in the 1950s and 1960s, the city carries on as a regional centre. New mining opportunities are being explored, tourist numbers continue to grow and renewable energy investments are being made. The Council and the community are building on their strengths to create jobs, and Broken Hill remains the town like no other.

Epilogue

Broken Hill's contributions to the country were gargantuan in the 20-year focus period of this book. The contributions were economic, social and environmental. They were tangible and intangible. The contributions came from a city that represented just 3 per cent of Australia's population.

Wealth creation arose principally from the value of mine output, valued at 32 million Australian pounds, in what may have been the peak year of 1956 (over AUD $1.25 billion today).[1] It was a large annual pie at around $1 billion per annum from which miners, shareholders, suppliers, government and the community could all take slices. Sheep grazing in the West Darling provided another source of wealth, with wool and sheep meat going to domestic and export markets.

WEALTH DISTRIBUTION

Broken Hill's mineral production generated significant export income to Australia as most of the silver, lead and zinc was exported. This came at a time when exports were badly needed as Australia was having trade balance issues with import growth exceeding export growth.

Miners were paid well and shared in high metal prices with the lead bonus amounting to half their wages on occasions. In 1956, the second highest year for lead bonus payments, lead bonus amounted to AUD $185 million paid to mine employees. There were times during the recession in 1961 when the lead bonus exceeded the value of shareholder dividends.[2] With half the people of Australia being paid the basic wage, a Broken Hill contract miner could earn over four times as much as a person on the basic wage. Miners were taxpayers as well and paid tax on the lead bonus received, as well as their salaries and wages.

Government at all levels laid claim to a share of the wealth created. Local government imposed high levies on the mines and the mines underwrote the Water Board's operation. The New South Wales government received royalties equal to about 10 per cent of mine profits. The Commonwealth Government weighed in with high levels of company tax and personal tax.

The mining companies paid dividends out of profits, invested in plant and equipment to remain competitive and had surplus funds available for investment in new mines and manufacturing. Their investment ended up making a significant contribution to Australia's mining and industrial development. Besides the Pilbara iron ore operations and Comalco, funded by CRA, were industrial operations funded by North Broken Hill, such as Associated Pulp and Paper Mills and Metal Manufactures Limited. Broken Hill South funded Alcoa's development and the Dutchess Phosphate mine.

Besides the unique payment of the lead bonus to mine employees, another distinguishing aspect of Broken Hill mining was the slice of the pie that was reinvested back into the community, enriching lives in the process. W.S. Robinson's desire to improve living conditions in Broken Hill from the mid 1930s found its full blossoming in the 1950s and 60s. It came to be known as corporate social responsibility. Broken Hill pioneered the effort to create a community consistent with long lived mines. The investment to create the regeneration area was unique. Providing funding for making Kinchega National Park had no precedents, nor did the purchase and gifting of artworks to the Art Gallery.

MINE LEADERSHIP EXPORTER

The minerals boom of the 1960s and early 1970s was only possible with well-trained mine managers. Broken Hill provided many of the managers for the new mines. Examples included Sir Russell Madigan, who became the head of

Hamersley Iron, the company that mined the Pilbara. Sir Frank Espie became a Director and Chairman of Bougainville Copper. No matter what mine you went to in Australia it was likely to have a mine manager trained in Broken Hill.

The mining diaspora from Broken Hill grew to dozens and dozens of leaders across Australia. Each made their mark, drawing on lessons learned and management practice from Broken Hill. They include Peter Coates from Zinc Corporation, where as underground manager at Metals Exploration's Nepean nickel mine near Coolgardie in Western Australia, he brought a focus on safety. Another is Vince Gauci. At the Woodlawn lead/zinc mine near Captain's Flat in New South Wales he innovated with shift length to reduce downtime and raise productivity, invoking the right to manage that he had seen compromised in Broken Hill.[3]

There were talented Broken Hill people outside mining who made important contributions to Australia as we have spotlighted. Few country towns could list an opera star, academics, inventors, doctors, broadcasters, sportspeople and a Federal court judge among their own.

MANAGEMENT PROCESSES

What also came out of Broken Hill were new management processes. In my mind they are as important as the tangible wealth creation. The practices turn out to have deep impact and are enduring to this day.

The collective bargaining model, with industrial agreements signed for three years, was finetuned in operation by the early 1950s. It delivered the mines' production goals and rapid productivity, safer working conditions and high pay for mine employees. When Mount Isa had strikes for eight months in 1964 and the New South Wales coalfields had frequent strikes, Broken Hill was unaffected.

Safer working conditions came about in several ways. One was by better risk assessment of unsafe conditions and practices. Another was by making shift bosses and mine managers accountable for the safety of men underground and on the surface. Data recording of accidents, sharing of data and learning from unsafe conditions and practices became the way to mine safely. Managers like John Ralph at CRA put safety in the forefront of change management. The realisation came that innovation in mining methods, front line manager accountability and better workforce management could improve safety *and* raise productivity. These innovations and many more in the Broken Hill mines were what is termed continuous improvement today. They paved the way for expectations of zero fatalities in a workplace, no matter how intrinsically unsafe it is, like underground mining.

The big difference between the first tumultuous decades of mining in Broken Hill and the postwar period was that reducing wages of miners and mine employees was off the table, regardless of inflation or falling metal prices. It left managers no choice but to maximize annual production and pull the productivity lever to keep the cost per ton of ore at levels that ensured profitable operations. This they did, and here lies the secret discovered in Broken Hill to remaining profitable during recessions without seeking to reduce mine employee wages.

Through the period 1950–70 high productivity growth occurred until the mid 1960s as ore tonnage each year increased while the number of mine employees fell due to natural attrition of 1–2 per cent per annum. This meant that the mines could remain profitable when metal prices fell by 25 per cent, as they did in 1958, without having to reduce costs per employee. The mines did reduce one shift per fortnight for a time in 1958, effectively lowering cost per employee.

Every large-scale mine around today treats employee costs as largely fixed and plans volumes that allow for a high profit margin and return on investment. Broken Hill mining companies showed how to manage for high annual production and productivity improvement, given the constraint of fixed wages for the three-year period of the Industrial Agreement.

In metallurgy Broken Hill mines had developed the flotation method for recovering zinc as a world leading technology in the early part of the twentieth century, an important contribution to Australia. Continuous improvement was made in metal recoveries. As an example, from 1950 to 1967 North Broken Hill held lead recovery at 97.4 per cent, silver increased from 92.1 to 94 per cent and zinc rose from 87.8 to 89 per cent.[4] At the other end of the line of lode Zinc Corporation was a leading-edge customer for the use of atomic absorption spectroscopy (AAS) in more accurately measuring zinc concentrates. Zinc Corporation's Bill Davis developed a new flotation cell, the Davcra cell. The mining and metallurgy industry globally benefited from these innovations.

THE NATURAL ENVIRONMENT

It took a long time for Broken Hill to come to grips with the destruction of the natural environment and the consequences of mining and overgrazing. Having a town that ran on wood in the early days meant there would most likely be a day of reckoning.

Overgrazing and rabbit plagues did their bit to contribute to sand drifts and dust storms. Overgrazing was addressed by stocking rate limits, imposed by the Western Lands Commission. Western Lands was the first Natural Resource Management Plan in Australia. Drought, rabbit plagues and goats had to be dealt with as part of grazing at the margins.

Out of this problem emerged a local solution, a regeneration area bigger than Sydney's CBD to stop sand drifts and ameliorate the effect of dust storms. The plan involved restoring natural vegetation by planting and keeping rabbits, sheep and goats out of the area. It was proposed by conservationists, funded by the mining companies and after proof of concept was established, endorsed and managed by the local council.

The regeneration initiative has been talked about, written about and trialled in other mine sites. Zinc Corporation managers who had been involved in the regeneration area trialled similar approaches at Mary Kathleen, the uranium mine in north Queensland, and at Comalco's bauxite operations at Weipa.[5]

The contribution to Australia came in several ways: first, in showing how conservationists and miners could work together around shared interests, including end of mine rehabilitation; second, in being a large-scale experiment to show how degraded land could be returned near to its natural state by removing threats; and third, in raising awareness about the environmental impact of new mines and how that can be mitigated.

Not only was Broken Hill a town like no other in Australia, but it made contributions to Australia that turned out to be nationally significant and lasting. The contributions were mostly economic from the rich line of lode but they also came from people and management practice. Achieving safety improvement together with productivity gains, alongside a more amenable environment, are accomplishments that resonate today as they did over half a century ago.

On my bookshelf is a book with a bright red cover, a radical manifesto called *The Industrial History of Broken Hill*, written by George Dale in 1918.[6] The people involved and the battles of 1892 and 1909 are described in detail. The book finishes before the long strike of 1919–20. If Dale had written his book 50 years later he would have had a lot of rewriting to do – of miner prosperity, far safer working conditions, of mining companies remaining profitable in recessions, of an engaged and thriving community that had few parallels. The reality became the 'beautiful history' that I have shared in this book.

Endnotes

Chapter 1

1. Hughes-Warrington, M., *History as Wonder: Beginning with Historiography*, Routledge, 2019.
2. The history of Broken Hill is well documented in books like Geoffrey Blainey's *The Rise of Broken Hill*, published by Melbourne University Press in 1968, Robert Solomon's coffee table book *The Richest Lode: Broken Hill 1883-1988*, published by Hale & Iremonger in 1988 and the volumes by local historian Ross Kearns. Jenny Camilleri's *Some Outstanding Women of Broken Hill and District*, published in 2002, fills an important gap. Bobbie Hardy's *West of the Darling*, Rigby,1969 and *Lament for the Barkindji*, Rigby, 1976, make important contributions to Broken Hill's regional position and the fate of the Indigenous people of the Darling River.
3. Schelling, T., *The Strategy of Conflict*, Harvard, 1960.

Chapter 2

1. B. Hardy, *West of the Darling*, Rigby, 1969.
2. R. Bridges, *From Silver to Steel: The Romance of the Broken Hill Proprietary*, George Robertson and Co,1920.
3. K. Koenig, *Broken Hill 100 Years of Mining*, New South Wales Department of Mineral Resources, 1983.
4. *Minerals of Broken Hill*, Ch 4, A, M & S Ltd, 1982.
5. G. Blainey, *The Rise of Broken Hill*, Macmillan, 1968.
6. R.J. Solomon, *The Richest Lode: Broken Hill 1883-1988*, Hale & Iremonger,1988.
7. G. Blainey, op. cit.
8. L. Curtis, *The History of Broken Hill: Its Rise and Progress*, Frearson's,1908.
9. R. Bridges, op. cit.
10. R. Kennedy, *Silver, Sin and Sixpenny Ale*, Melbourne University Press,1978.
11. L. Curtis, op. cit.
12. G. Blainey, op. cit.
13. Ibid.
14. W.S. Robinson, *If I Remember Rightly*, F.W. Cheshire,1967.
15. B. Ellem and J. Shields, *Eugene Patrick O'Neill*, Australian Dictionary of Biography, 2005.
16. *Barrier Daily Truth*, 18 June 1954 (https://trove.nla.gov.au/newsper/article/139970313).
17. W.S. Robinson, op. cit.
18. Ibid.
19. G. Blainey, op. cit.

Chapter 3

1. Mine employees of 6459 from Shields' paper, compared with 5917 estimate by Nixon based on MMA data. The numbers were peak employment. J. Shields, 'Lead Bonus Happy: Profit Sharing, Productivity and Industrial Relations in the Broken Hill Mining Industry, 1925–83', *Australian Economic History Review*, November 1997. J. Nixon, A Bit about Mining, unpublished presentation, May 2024, provided to Robert McLean.
2. On 30 January 1953 the *Sydney Morning Herald* reported that 'In Broken Hill today there is roughly a car to every family. With a population of 32,000, the city has 12,000 motor vehicle registrations, which is a higher proportion than in the State of New York. That is a fair indication of Broken Hill's prosperity.'
3. Productivity Commission, *Assessing Australia's Productivity Performance*, p 12 estimates Australia labour productivity grew at 2.6 per cent per annum from 1964–65 to 1968–69.
4. J. Camilleri, *Some Outstanding Women of Broken Hill and District*, Broken Hill Historical Society, 2002.
5. Ibid.
6. R.H.B. Kearns, *Broken Hill 1940-73*, Broken Hill Historical Society,1976.

Chapter 4

1. Barkindji Elder Badger Bates, Maitland Regional Art Gallery interview, 2019.
2. B. Hardy, *West of the Darling*, Rigby, 1969.
3. B. Hardy, *Lament for the Barkindji*, Rigby, 1976.
4. R. Bridges, *From Silver to Steel*, George Robertson & Co, 1920.

5. G. Blainey, *The Rise of Broken Hill*, Macmillan of Australia, 1968.
6. R. Solomon, *The Richest Lode: Broken Hill 1883-1988*, Hale & Iremonger, 1988.
7. DOC4568, towardstruth.org.au, 22 January 2025.
8. J. Thompson, *Immigration into the Barrier Ranges After 1875*, Museums of History (Sydney), 2023.
9. Interview with Beryl Carmichael, *The Australian Women's Register*, http://www.womenaustralia.info.
10. Tara Callaghan interview with Badger Bates, Maitland Regional Art Gallery, 2017.
11. S. Martin, *Report for New South Wales Public Works on the Broken Hill Courthouse*, 2023.
12. Alan Whicker, *Walled City*, Yorkshire Television, 1970.
13. M. Withers, *Bushmen of the Great Anabranch*, self-published,1989.
14 Conversation with Dr Deb Nias, 23 May 2025.
15 Murray Darling Basin Commission, *Menindee Fish Deaths*, 18 September 2023.
16. M. Mallen-Cooper and B. Zampatti, 'Restoring the ecological integrity of a dryland river: Why low flows in the Barwon-Darling River must flow', *Ecological Management & Restoration*, 16 September 2020.
17. R. Solomon, op. cit.
18. M. Withers, op. cit.
19. Ibid.
20. Anabranch Water, *Inquiry into Water Augmentation*, Submission No. 32, NSW Parliament, 9 August 2016.
21. L. Leslie and M. Speer, 'Climate Change Reduces Darling River Water by Decreasing Australian Rainfall', *Journal of Water*, Vol. 1, Issue No. 3, 2024.

Chapter 5

1. B. Hardy, *West of the Darling*, Rigby,1967.
2 M. Withers, *Bushmen of the Great Anabranch*, self published, 1989.
3. J. Blackwell, *Woolcunda Station: A Century of Shepherding*, self-published, 2017.

Chapter 6

1. W.S. Robinson, *If I Remember Rightly*, F.W. Cheshire,1967.
2. L. Pearce, *Kinship: Belonging in a World of Relations*, Center for Humans and Nature Press, 2021.
3. M. Morris, 'Plant Regeneration in the Broken Hill District', *Australian Journal of Science*, Vol. 2, Issue 2,1939.
4. Ibid.
5. P. Ardil, *Albert Morris and the Broken Hill Regeneration Area: Time, Landscape and Renewal*, aabr.org.au, 2017.
6. H. Webber, *The Greening of the Hill*, Hyland House,1992.
7. P. Ardill, op. cit.
8. H. Webber, op. cit.
9. Ibid.
10. M. Annandale, J. Meadows, P. Erskine, 'Indigenous forest livelihoods and bauxite mining: A case study from Northern Australia', Article 113014, *Journal of Environmental Management*, Vol. 294, 15 September 2021.

Chapter 7

1. The ability to hold profit margins when metal prices fall requires that you lower the cost per ton of ore produced. You can do this by lowering the cost per mine employee or increasing productivity measured by tons per employee. For the technically minded, cost per ton of ore = cost per

mine employee divided by tons of ore per mine employee (productivity). Reducing wages to lower the cost per employee was not an option because of the experience of the past. Productivity turned out to be a hugely impactful lever to reduce mining cost per ton of ore and increase competitiveness.

2. O. Woodward, *A Review of the Broken Hill Lead-Silver-Zinc Industry*, Australian Institute of Mining and Metallurgy,1965.
3. R.H.B. Kearns, *Broken Hill*, Vol. 4, Broken Hill Historical Society,1976.
4. Personal communication with John Ralph.
5. Private communication with Frank McLean, MM.
6. The quote by Sir Frank Espie was that 'The union leaders were as honourable as the mine management and were good men to deal with' in R. Solomon, *The Richest Lode*, Hale and Iremonger, 1988. Andrew Fairweather's concern for miners' safety is noted by B. Carroll, *Built On Silver: A History of Broken Hill South*, Hill of Content Publishing,1986.
7. K. Tsokhas, *Beyond Dependence*, Oxford University Press,1986.
8. Ibid.
9. Barton Maughan is quoted in the Yorkshire television program *Whicker's World*, 1970, accessible on YouTube.
10 W.A. Howard, *Barrier Bulwark: The Life and Times of Shorty O'Neil*, Wiley, 1990.

Chapter 8

1. W.S. Robinson, *If I Remember Rightly*, Cheshire,1967.
2. Ibid.
3. Ibid.
4. *Sydney Morning Herald*, 30 January 1953.

5. See the chapter on industrial agreements in O.H. Woodward, *A Review of the Broken Hill Silver Lead Zinc Industry,* Australian Institute of Mining and Metallurgy, 1965.
6. *Sydney Morning Herald*, 30 January 1953.
7. K. Koenig, *Broken Hill 100 Years of Mining*, NSW Department of Mineral Resources,1983.
8. J. Shields, 'Lead Bonus Happy: Profit Sharing, Productivity and Industrial Relations in the Broken Hill Mining Industry,1925-83', *Australian Economic History*, Vol. 37, No. 3, 1997.
9. R. Porter, *Rio Tinto in Australia: The Origins and Formation of an International Resources Company 1954-1995*, Connor Court Publishing, 2024.
10. O.H. Woodward, op. cit.
11. R.J. Solomon, *The Richest Lode: Broken Hill 1883-1988*, Hale & Iremonger,1988.
12. O.H. Woodward, op. cit.
13. R. Porter, op. cit.
14. S. Kaplan, *The Enduring Wisdom of Milton Friedman,* www.promarket.org

Chapter 9

1. S. Goodman, *The Fatal Lodes – Mining Deaths in the Broken Hill District*, Broken Hill City Council, 2012.
2. Migration Heritage Centre, New South Wales, Belongings Interviews.
3. S. Goodman, op. cit.
4. Ibid.
5. *Barrier Daily Truth*, 8 February 1950 (accessed on Trove).
6. O.H. Woodward, *A Review of the Broken Hill Lead-Silver-Zinc Industry*, Australian Institute of Mining and Metallurgy,1965.

7. Ibid.
8. A fatality from carbon monoxide poisoning following a firing occurred at Broken Hill South in 1961.
9. R.J. Solomon, op. cit.
10. O.H. Woodward, op. cit.

Chapter 10

1. *Whicker's World*, Yorkshire Television, 1970, accessible on YouTube.
2. R.H.B. Kearns, *Broken Hill 1940-73*, Broken Hill Historical Society, 1976.
3. Ibid.
4. W.A. Howard, *Barrier Bulwark: The Life and Times of Shorty O'Neil*, Willry,1990.
5. Yorkshire Television, *Walled City*,1970.
6. B. Bottom, 'Behind the Barrier', *The Bulletin*, Vol. 185, No. 4347, 1963.
7. W.A. Howard, op. cit.
8. Ibid.

Chapter 11

1. B. Kennedy, *Silver, Sin and Sixpenny Ale*, Melbourne University Press,1978.
2. K. Mannix, *Jews of the Outback: Jewish Settlement in Broken Hill*, University of Sydney, http://handle.net/2123/17234
3. NSW Migration Heritage Centre, 2006.
4. Personal correspondence with John Santich, September 2025.
5. E. McInerney, *Pubs, Publicans and People of Broken Hill and the Far West*, Broken Hill Book Company, 2024.
6. R. Ravlich, *Skywriting*, Brandl & Schlesinger, 2019.

7. Personal correspondence with Deidre Hardy (nee Kolinac), 2024.

Chapter 12

1. R. Putnam, *Bowling Alone, The Collapse and Revival of American Community*, Simon and Schuster, 2000.
2. *Barrier Daily Truth*, 19 March 1954.
3. R.H.B. Kearns, *Broken Hill 1940-73*, Broken Hill Historical Society,1976.
4. Memoirs of Frank McLean MM.
5. R. Putnam, op. cit.
6. R. Kearns, op. cit.

Chapter 13

1. Personal communication with Hester Lyon, Founding Co-director, Slag Heap Projects.
2. Wikipedia, Florence May Harding, en.wikipedia.org.
3. https://www.visitbrokenhill.com/Discover/Heroes-Larrrikins-Visionaries-Trail/Visual-artists (accessed 8 February 2025).
4. A. Newman, anart4life.com, 7 October 2020.
5. J. Camilleri, *In the Broken Hill Paddock*, self published, 2002.
6. Ibid.
7. https://trove.nla.gov.au/newspaper/article/44347733, 8 January 2025.
8. https://www.abc.net.au/news/dark-history-behind-Broken Hill's-most-valuable painting, 10 January 2018.

Chapter 14

1. J. Camilleri, *Some Outstanding Women of Broken Hill and District*, Broken Hill Historical Society, 2002.

2. Quoted in R Ravlich's book *Skywriting*, Brandl & Schlesinger, 2019, p. 43.
3. Ibid.
4. Personal communication, 2024.
5. Personal communication,12 January 2025.

Chapter 15

1. W. Stegner, *On Teaching and Writing Fiction*, Penguin, 2002.
2. *Australian Women's Register* (2025), Teresa Alfonsi, https://www.womenaustralia.info/, (accessed 22 August 2025).
3. Personal correspondence with Serge Caplygin, 20 June 2025.
4. Personal communication with Helen Palmer, 28 June 2025.
5. G. Brennan and J. Buchanan, *The Power to Tax: Analytical Foundations of a Fiscal Constitution*, Cambridge University Press,1980.
6. G. Brennan and J. Buchanan, *The Reason of Rules: Constitutional Political Economy*, Cambridge University Press,1985.
7. J. Buchanan, *Better than Plowing and Other Personal Essays*, University of Chicago Press,1992.
8. https://www.abc.net.au/rn_RobynRavlic%20interview.mp3
9. R. Ravlich, *Skywriting: Making Radio Waves*, Brandl & Schlesinger, 2019.

Chapter 16

1 Solomon, R.J., *The Richest Lode: Broken Hill 1883-1988,* Hale and Iremonger,1988

2 Ibid.

3 https://economy.id.com.au/broken-hill, accessed 24 September 2025.

4 Ibid

5 https://www.benevolent.org.au, 26 September 2023, accessed 24 September 2025.
6 https://www.hydrostor.ca, 14 November 2024, accessed 24 September 2025.
7 https://www.abc.net.au/news, 17 September 2025, accessed 24 September 2025.

Epilogue

1 Report of the Department of Mines for 1956, https://nswdpe.intersearch.com.au/nswdpejspui/handle/1/2586
2 Ibid.
3 Personal communications, October 2025.
4 M. Bohm and T. Slattery, Ore Concentrations Practice at North Broken Hill Limited, Broken Hill Mines – 1968, AIMM.
5 H. Webber, *The Greening of the Hill*, Hyland House, 1992.
6 G. Dale, *The Industrial History of Broken Hill*, Fraser and Jenkinson, 1918.

Acknowledgements

I'm new to writing history. I've read many history books and love the grand sweep of authors who write with a narrative style, authors like Geoffrey Blainey, Barbara Tuchman or William Dalrymple. I have had to learn to write a narrative style that tells a story, quite unlike the experience I've had writing business books. I have one person to thank for that, my wife and editor Paula McLean who has pushed my thinking and writing with the most probing question, 'What are you trying to convey to the reader, Rob?' What, indeed! Paula, your questions and suggestions have been ever so important in helping me blend memoir with social and economic history.

I wish to acknowledge and thank Ginny Grant, my daughter and Publisher of Bakers Lane Books, for taking on a novice history writer. You have encouraged me and backed me in this project. Dave Grant has brought his superb design skills to the book cover and the map of the surrounds of Broken Hill. My love and deepest gratitude to you both.

I have had access to my father Frank McLean's memoir and essays he wrote about life in Broken Hill for the period from 1918–77, apart from years in war service and being posted to BHP's Whyalla shipyard from 1940–50. I thank my sister Judith Felgenhaur who typed and assembled our father's memoir and essays. I also wish to acknowledge the encouragement of my brother Ian McLean to write the book and share family history. My one remaining relative still living in Broken Hill, Helen Giblett, contributed many stories and memories of this time.

Two historians influenced the book I've written. One is Marnie Hughes Warrington with her book *History as Wonder.* Marnie's book encouraged me to be curious and ask questions, to marshal facts and analysis to support the hypothesis, then to tell the story. I was given Geoffrey Blainey's *The Rise of Broken Hill* in 1968 by close friends at my farewell when I left to study in the US. Geoffrey Blainey has generously provided permission to use quotes in several places. As well, I thank Robert Porter for his quote permissions.

Although not an historian, Robyn Ravlich wrote a note to me about 'our beautiful history', referring to our time growing up in South Broken Hill in the 1950s and 60s, being part of a thriving community and being well educated at Alma Public and Broken Hill High School. Robyn's phrase stuck with me and led me to define these years in a different way, where education, the contributions of migrant communities and voluntary organisations enriched the social capital of Broken Hill.

As well as drawing on my father's memoirs, many texts, research papers, newspapers, census data and interviews, there are many people with lived experience I've had the opportunity to learn from and test my thinking on.

I wish to thank those I spoke to about how the mines were run. They included John Ralph AC, Leigh Clifford AO, Peter Coates AO, Vince Gauci, John Dini, Roger Massy-Greene AM, Bill Hardy and Jeff Nixon. Jeff shared his deep knowledge of Broken Hill mining from the numerous presentations he has given.

My classmates from Broken Hill High School helped with facts and stories about our distinguished class. I wish to thank Leslie Bills, Helen Palmer, Ian Wright, Peter Perry and Merran Neville.

For insight about the Barka Darling and Indigenous people I wish to thank Sarah Martin, Badger Bates, Fiona Kelly and Peter Jinks. Ross Leddra (who died in 2025) shared his experience from the Darling River Action Group with me the year before, in 2024. Vic Seekamp of Woolcunda station reviewed the chapter on grazing in the West Darling for me and I thank her for her contributions.

My friends Deidre Hardy and John Santich contributed their perspectives on their migrant family history. Another friend, Jeff Paynter, helped me understand the rich range of community organisations in Broken Hill. My neighbour

Sandra Kanck provided perspectives of women in Broken Hill from her family experience. Stephen Hywood, a South Football Club star, filled in gaps for me on the role of footy in the community. Serge Caplygin filled in detail on his brother Dimitri's stellar career. Margaret Kearns and Lance Leslie shared experiences on how supportive the Broken Hill environment was to their careers.

I wish to thank Jen Thompson and Pam Harding for giving permission to use the May Harding painting *Broken Hill Nocturne* for the cover of the book. I'd also like to thank Kathryn Graham of the Broken Hill City Art Gallery for her support and arranging permissions. Hester Lyon at Slag Heap Projects, which advocate for Far West NSW artists, first drew my attention to May Harding's pivotal role in Broken Hill becoming the art capital of the outback. ABC Radio Broken Hill's Andrew Schmidt has been very supportive of the book project as has Robynne Sanderson at Under the Silver Tree bookshop and I want to thank them both.

I also wish to thank copyeditor Annabel Adair and publicist Julia Ferracane for their support in this project.

Memories fade with events that occurred more than fifty years ago, but in telling this beautiful history, the picture became clear again. For me, and thousands of others, Broken Hill remains the town like no other.

Index

Index